God Said It,
Don't Sweat It

God Said It, Don't Sweat It

How to Keep Life's Petty Hassles from Overwhelming You

NEIL CLARK WARREN

THOMAS NELSON PUBLISHERS
Nashville

Contents

CONTENTS

❦

Contents

CONTENTS

Contents

Acknowledgments

ROLF ZETTERSTEN, Publisher at Thomas Nelson and my close friend, came up with the idea for this book. Moreover, he has been the driving force behind every stage of its development.

Countless other people have made significant contributions. The most important contribution was made by my editor and friend, Keith Wall. He became my valued partner in every aspect of the writing.

Sue Braden, my administrative assistant, performed magnificently, as usual, in the preparation of the manuscript.

Curtis Lundgren and Cindy Blades at Thomas Nelson have been thoughtful and sensitive partners in this project.

As I read through these writings, I realize how much I owe my family, friends, students, and clients for their stimulating interactions and unique contributions to my thinking and development.

But as you move through the book, you will see that my dad, Otis James Warren, stands at the top of the list. He clearly was my life model, even during those years when I wasn't emotionally secure enough to admit it, and my gratitude to him is immense. I joyfully dedicate this collection of essays to him.

Introduction

IF YOU ARE searching for effective ways to master the daily challenges of life, look to God. He is committed to helping you experience contentment and joy at the center of yourself. And He tells you how to deal with your everyday concerns so they will become as inconsequential as a little dust on your furniture. If your life needs some friendly guidance and instruction, mixed with plenty of inspiration and encouragement, God is more than willing to provide it.

In the New Testament, the apostle Paul is unbelievably proficient and persuasive at communicating God's deepest thoughts about life's most perplexing issues.

All of the essays in this book are based upon Paul's four letters to the churches at Galatia, Ephesus, Philippi, and Colossae. In these short epistles, which were probably written between A.D. 58 and 61, Paul deals with matters that range from friendship to marriage, from ways to break free from sin's grip to becoming a new and different person. He directly addresses how to tame your temper, control your tongue, and open your mind. He teaches you how to become more like Christ, how to take a big interest in other people, how to overflow with prayer for others, how to be kind and tenderhearted, and, most of all, how to get into a right relationship with Him.

During the years that Paul spent writing these letters, he undoubtedly was in jail. He probably had at least a chain around his wrist or ankle, and the conditions under which he lived were far from optimal. Adding to his difficulties was the necessity that he dictate these letters to someone else. He had to rely on willing but slow transmission of his magnificent ideas.

But in each of the letters, Paul's ideas soar to the heavens. They plumb the very heart of God. They penetrate the deepest and most profound aspects of the Christian faith.

If we integrate these ideas into our lives, we will inevitably manage our problems and challenges more effectively, live our moments more joyfully, handle our marriages more skillfully, raise our children more wisely, and experience a closeness in all of our relationships that will vitalize our days.

I can personally testify to the power of these teachings. For thirty-three years, I have worked with persons in the intimate relationship of psychotherapy. I have observed every kind of problem, and I have tried to help individuals who have suffered from various difficulties and painful experiences. The apostle Paul's answers to these dilemmas—taken, as it were, straight from God's lips—have a thorough and extraordinary way of solving complex and puzzling problems.

What I do in this book is simply select eighty five small and large issues that present themselves to most of us on a daily basis—and then let God speak powerfully and convincingly in relation to each of them.

I hope you will experience as much inspiration as I have, and I hope you'll find as many solutions for your problems as you read these essays as I discovered for my problems during the writing of them.

I also hope you will feel the bondedness to me that I felt to you as I worked these matters through. And I hope your sense of appreciation for the apostle Paul will become equal to my own. He was a great man of God, and if he were writing this Introduction, he would surely end with something like this: "The rich blessings of our Lord Jesus Christ be upon your lives."

1

Don't Worry About Anything, but Pray About Everything

THE APOSTLE PAUL encourages us not to worry about anything. In one broad stroke, he models a mastery over the "small stuff" that is backed up by a specific instruction unavailable to those outside the powerful faith he promotes.

Paul says simply, "Pray about everything!"

Paul teaches us that worry isn't worth the effort. Goodness knows, worry requires a lot of effort. I once heard a person say, "A day of worry is more exhausting than a day of work." And someone else has said that "worry is wasting today's time cluttering up tomorrow's opportunities with yesterday's troubles."

Most things you worry about never live up to their fear-causing power. One recent survey indicates that 40 percent of the things we worry about never happen, 30 percent are in the past and can't be changed, 12 percent concern the affairs of others that aren't our business, 10 percent involve real or imagined sickness, and 8 percent are worth worrying about.

But Paul tells us that even the 8 percent of "legitimate" worries aren't really worth worrying about. Why? Because we have the God of the universe on our side, and He offers to carry our worries for us.

So, Paul says, put your energy where it can really do some good. Pray passionately about whatever it is that concerns you!

As a psychotherapist for the past thirty years, I have watched thousands of men and women go through perilous times. I have noted on many occasions that those who pray passionately end up overcoming the difficulties they face. They bring a "mighty power" to the issues they confront, and this power does incredible things in and through them.

When I was in high school, I encountered an inspirational man named Dr. Cherry Parker, who wrote a book entitled *Prayer Can Change Your Life.* Through his encouragement, I began praying about the things that concerned me. For a long time, however, I remained unconvinced that prayer could really change things. I sometimes prayed about minor matters, but nothing unusual seemed to happen. Prayer for me was kind of a "ho-hum" experience.

But when I later discovered "passionate prayer," I realized how powerful the process of prayer can be in the life of a human being. Passionate prayer, or "fervent" prayer, is very different from "mechanical" or "perfunctory" prayer. It almost always pertains to something that is of great importance to you. You pray with tremendous emotional involvement. Whatever it is that you care *deeply* about, the absolute best thing you can do for it is pray passionately. Turn your attention to the source of incredible power. Ask God to move through you in relation to your concern.

You will come to the place where worry will literally vanish from your life. When you encounter a challenge, you will immediately begin to pray. This new perspective will make you a dynamic person, because the Holy Spirit will empower you to do great things.

No more worry—just prayer!

Don't worry about anything; instead,
pray about everything.

PHILIPPIANS 4:6

2

Focus on Doing Good, and Watch Your Life Get Better and Better

WHEN TIMES ARE frustrating and you wonder how you're going to make it through this ordeal or that one, it's crucial to keep your best goals carefully focused. The apostle Paul constantly reminds us that the healthiest goal we can have is to *do good*. Paul makes it clear time after time that "doing good" involves focusing on the needs and problems of other people.

It is a fundamental psychological truth that when you help other people with their most pressing issues, it won't be long until you feel significantly better about yourself.

I'll never forget the time I took my friend Harold Graham to play golf. Though he was an outstanding athlete at our college, he made no pretense about being a golfer. In fact, he'd never set foot on a golf course before that day.

On the first tee we were joined by two older men who were seasoned golfers. They were dressed immaculately, and their golf equipment was expensive and stylish. When they both hit their drives far out on that first hole, Harold gave me a wary look. He rummaged through his old bag and fished out three or four balls. They were all driving range balls with a bright orange band around them. As the other gentlemen exchanged glances, I hurried over to lend Harold one of my new balls . . . which he proceeded to hit into a nearby bush. After five minutes of searching for the ball, we gave up. I helped him tee up another ball . . . which he dribbled about twenty feet.

And that's the way it went for eighteen holes. My entire focus that day was on helping Harold do what he needed to do to avoid embarrassment and enjoy himself. I gently offered some pointers, lent him my clubs, gave him lots of encouragement, and kept the mood light so he could laugh at his struggles rather than feel miserable.

To my amazement, when the scores were tallied at the end of the round, I had the best score I'd ever achieved on that course. I had been so absorbed in helping my friend that I'd been freed from the worry and anxiety that would have diminished my own performance. Serving and assisting Harold enabled my own abilities to reach new heights.

Every part of life needs to be like that! One of my heroes, John Wesley, once wrote:

> Do all the good you can,
> By all the means you can,
> In all the ways you can,

In all the places you can,
At all the times you can,
To all the people you can,
As long as ever you can.

When you keep your mind focused on serving others, you create the freedom to function at your best. Remember this secret when times are hardest. It all revolves around doing good, and when we do good, our lives begin to soar.

*Make the most of every opportunity
you have for doing good.*

EPHESIANS 5:16

3

Do Your Best and Don't Compare Yourself with Others

ONE OF LIFE'S unexpected contradictions is this: when we compare ourselves to other people, we inevitably end up performing at a significantly lower level. Granted, we sometimes feel better about ourselves for a short period, but when we become convinced that we can boost our self-esteem only if we perform better than someone else, we become distracted. We take our eyes off the real goal, and we lose our focus. We end up spending far too much energy thinking about the persons with whom we are competing. We almost always lose the internal reward we so passionately pursue.

It was through the writings of psychoanalyst Freda Fromm Reichman I first learned that comparisons lead to feelings of both inferiority and superiority—but seldom produce emotional health. Show me a person who feels inferior, and I will show you a person who secretly feels superior to someone else. Hidden just below that attitude of superiority, there is almost always some inferiority. These feelings of inferiority and superiority usually lead to internal turmoil and demoralization that rob of us of our sense of true worth. They severely reduce the freedom we experience, and certainly diminish our performance.

On the other hand, when we focus our attention on *self*-improvement—on doing our best—a totally different inner dynamic takes over. We always have our own personal best. No one can ever take it away except us. When we simply give our all, without the distraction of comparisons, we can delight in becoming more efficient, skillful, or productive.

The fact is, comparisons are counterproductive and meaningless. Since each of us has a brain with two billion megabytes of capacity, and since each person's brain allows him or her to do some things better and some things worse than others, figuring out an honest and helpful basis for true comparisons becomes impossible. Only God knows. That is, you may be significantly better than I am in something because you are blessed with natural talent. But, I may be better than you in some other area. Why should we compare ourselves? Especially since this comparison obscures our more reasonable goal—to do our best.

The apostle Paul says it so clearly: Do your best and don't compare yourself with others. If you will follow this advice, your "best" will get better and better and better. You will be able to applaud other people's bests, even if they are considerably better than yours. This is an eternal secret that will maximize your performance, minimize your anxiety, and greatly enrich all your relationships.

Let everyone be sure that he is doing his very best,
for then he will have the personal satisfaction
of work well done, and won't need to
compare himself with someone else.

GALATIANS 6:4

4

See Yourself for Who You Are—and Watch Your Relationships Soar

WITHOUT A DOUBT, the key to contented living and satisfying relationships is the recognition that perfection is never a criterion for worth and value. So if you have some imperfections, let them become apparent—and then get about the task of growing your way through them.

I have watched hundreds of persons in my counseling office deal with this time-honored principle. When they think that their value as individuals hinges on being perfect, they engage in an endless process of hiding their flaws and defending their actions.

But when these folks finally get in touch with the gospel truth that they are supremely lovable—that they can never be more or less lovable than they are right now—they can begin discovering themselves at the deepest levels and becoming all that God intended them to be. It all begins with knowing how wonderfully loved they are, how free they are from the need for perfection.

In any relationship between marriage partners or friends, family members or coworkers, the person who gains a clear perspective on herself or himself is always viewed as the healthiest, the most attractive, the one everyone wants to be around.

Why is this so? Because these people create an atmosphere of honesty and acceptance. Because they can admit their deficiencies and areas that need to be developed, they make it possible for others to deal openly with their own struggles and problems. Because they do not present themselves as flawless, they remove the pressure and threat of standards that must be lived up to and expectations that must be met.

Is anyone perfect? No, not anyone on earth. Only God is perfect! And you don't need to be God—not in your own appraisal of yourself or in relation to anybody. You are free to simply be you.

There will always be aspects of you that fall short of some idealized goal. As you are able to recognize and accept these aspects, you will have a chance to modify them and improve them. And you will set other people free to do the same kind of growing.

Each of us must bear
some faults and burdens of his own.
For none of us is perfect!

GALATIANS 6:5

5

Live Your Life to the Fullest

As a psychologist, I have become convinced that the fundamental motivation for all of us is the need to feel good about who we are. Most of the time, though, we are so familiar with our deficiencies, weaknesses, and frailties that we feel unlovable. Somehow we sense that to be lovable, we need to deserve it, and we find it impossible to think of ourselves as deserving.

The New Testament is all about helping us feel good about ourselves. It says that our lives will change profoundly when we understand as best we can God's complete and unrestrained love for us. The apostle Paul encourages us to let ourselves feel and experience how long, how wide, how deep, and how high the Father's love for us really is. Paul says when we embrace this freely offered love, we will be filled with God Himself!

At this point, God's mighty power will be at work within us, and unbelievable things will begin to happen. In fact, Paul says things that happen in our lives will be far beyond our deepest prayers, desires, thoughts, or hopes. Greater than our dreams! Beyond anything that we have ever imagined!

Our situation or station in life doesn't matter. What matters is that we get in touch with this love for ourselves. When we do, everything about our existence will take on a totally different quality. Our lives will be transfused with the deep joy that God intends for us. Our sufferings will be manageable. Our problems will be well within our ability to handle them.

If you are like I am, you love surprises. The greatest surprise you will ever experience is the surprising joy that comes when God, through His Holy Spirit, fills your heart to the fullest. Your days will be filled with more than you would ever ask or even dream of.

Now glory be to God who by his mighty
power at work within us is able to do far more
than we would ever dare to ask or even dream of—
infinitely beyond our highest prayers,
desires, thoughts, or hopes.

EPHESIANS 3:20

6

Be Patient with Each Other

IT WAS RAINING cats and dogs in southern California, and I was scheduled to conduct a seminar that night in Portland, Oregon. When I arrived at the L.A. airport, I was met by huge crowds, long lines, and cramped corridors. Then things got worse. The PA system announced that my flight was "delayed"—a word that fills any air traveler with fear and frustration.

"We're waiting for the plane to arrive from Phoenix," a harried airline attendant told me, "but it can't land because of the storm."

"Are there any other flights going to Portland?" I asked.

"No," a second attendant replied curtly. "We'll let everyone know as soon as we get more information. In the meantime, you'll just have to wait."

The dozen or so people standing behind me groaned, grumbled, and sighed irritably.

I groaned, too. Thinking of the hundreds of people who

would be waiting for me in Portland, I felt the knot in my stomach tighten and my blood pressure soar.

I started to say something pointed, but then I remembered Paul's words: "Be patient with each other, making allowance for each other's faults because of your love."

In the course of a second or two, a silent conversation flashed through my mind. *I can gripe and complain and throw a fit, but what's that going to accomplish?* I told myself. *Since there's nothing you can do, shrug it off and don't make things worse than they are.*

I simply nodded to the attendant, walked away from the ticket counter, took my seat on the floor with the mass of humanity in the middle of the terminal—and waited patiently. I met some fellow passengers who were sitting on the floor beside me. For the next few hours, we talked and laughed together. We swapped stories and jokes, resolving to make the best of a bad situation.

That evening when I got to Portland in time to give my presentation, I remembered the magic of the apostle's words. I had been patient with my fellow human beings, and the time had passed rapidly.

The next time you choose the bank window with the trainee who seems to take forever, be patient. The next time you get stuck behind the slowest of slowpokes on the freeway, take a deep breath. The next time someone races to get ahead of you at the grocery store checkout, smile and let it go. Patience is a wonderful thing for both the person you're upset with and for you. But *especially* for you!

*Be patient with each other, making allowance for
each other's faults because of your love.*

EPHESIANS 4:2

7

Keep Your Heart
and Mind Open

LEE EDWARD TRAVIS was the greatest human being I ever met. Dr. Travis, the Dean of the Graduate School of Psychology at Fuller Seminary where I taught for many years, constantly impressed me with his zeal for learning, openness to fresh insights, and receptiveness to new ways of doing things. I doubt anyone ever heard him say, "We've *always* done it this way" or "We can't do that—it's never been done!"

In fact, when he was in his early nineties, Dr. Travis's mind and heart remained wide open to new understandings and "new truths." Even at that advanced age, he delighted in mastering some new skill or studying an unexplored subject. He never allowed his mind to grow stagnant.

If we want to manage the problems and challenges of life—and manage them exceedingly well—we will make sure our hearts and minds are open every day. Since the secret of great living always starts with our getting into a right relationship with God, we will especially open ourselves to what He wants us to learn about His complex universe.

When we think we have a *full* understanding of something, we risk shutting ourselves off from a new aspect or angle that might enrich our understanding. If we believe that we have "all the truth," we may arrogantly proceed through our lives in the face of facts that would change our lives considerably.

When I am trying to assess people's emotional health, I always consider how open they are to growth and change. If I determine that their defenses have developed thick walls around them—walls designed for protection but walls that will likely cause stagnation—I know immediately that their primary relationships are bound to suffer.

The future belongs to the people who stay open, receptive, and curious. Of all our human resources, the most precious is the desire to improve. The writer of Proverbs says it well: "The intelligent man is always open to new ideas. In fact, he looks for them" (18:15).

It all starts with getting ourselves into an intimate, personal relationship with the one true God who knows us far better than we know ourselves, loves us far more freely than we could ever imagine, and always has new things to show us and teach us. It is this relationship and this openness that will provide the stimulation and excitement that make every day more rewarding.

❧

*They are far away from the life of God
because they have shut their minds against him,
and they cannot understand his ways.*

EPHESIANS 4:18

8

Do Only What Is Good
and Right and True

IT WAS RED AUERBACH, longtime coach and general manager of the fabled Boston Celtics, who said, "Show me a good loser, and I'll show you a loser!" For Red Auerbach, the name of the game was *winning*.

My mother, Rosa Clark Warren, exposed me to a totally different philosophy: "It isn't whether you win or lose that counts; it's how you play the game."

I have ricocheted between Red Auerbach and my mother all my life. Sometimes I obsess over winning, but sometimes I focus on my effort and quality of living. How about you?

When I'm on the highway, I often feel as if I'm in an auto race. When one car zips by me and leaves me in the dust, I sometimes hear my mother. But when too many cars pass me by, the Red Auerbach in me takes over. My need to win and not to be a "loser" suddenly dominates in my life.

The apostle Paul cuts through all of this and says, "Do only what is good and right and true" because you *are* a winner! You don't need to be faster than anyone, accumulate more worldly goods, achieve more earthly status, or secure the favor of important people. Paul essentially says, "Let go of all that nonsense and concentrate on doing what you know is good and right."

The secret is to get yourself planted deeply in Christ's love for you. When you have this kind of abundant affection always available, you don't need to earn your worth in any other way. It sets you free to drive the freeways of your life at a safe and prudent speed. You accumulate worldly goods only when necessary. You dispense with the furious quest to boost your image. You have no hunger for what will give you only a few seconds of happiness.

Rather, you delight in every moment because you know that the big issues of your life have all been resolved in a satisfying way. You wake up in the morning, engage in your activities, and go to sleep at night fully assured that you are a winner—regardless of external factors. You are set free to live that life best characterized as "good and right and true."

Because of this light within you, you should do
only what is good and right and true.

EPHESIANS 5:9

9

Always Give Thanks
for Everything

IF YOU GET your attitude right, your life will be a thousand times more enjoyable. For instance, if you wake up in the morning and focus on all the things that are exciting and meaningful in your life, your energy level will be high. You will be eager to meet the day head-on.

William James, one of America's most insightful psychologists, put it succinctly: "It is our attitude at the beginning of a difficult undertaking which, more than anything else, will determine its successful outcome."

Focus on the positive in your life, and you will automatically become more appreciative, more joyful, more thankful. Life will take on brighter colors.

Everybody loves being around positive people—people who find the good in each situation and in each person they encounter. Even the person who develops these positive attitudes enjoys being around himself significantly more.

My close friend Dr. Lewis Smedes, a professor of social ethics and the author of many acclaimed books, recently put it to me concisely and pointedly: "Gratitude is at the very heart of contentment. My sense of satisfaction in life springs from the feeling of gratitude. I have never met a truly thankful, appreciative person who is not happy. So close are gratitude and contentment that I would equate them."

What I keep discovering about myself and the people in my life is that gratitude and affirmation raise the richness of our interactions to the highest possible level. The apostle Paul put it best: "Start by giving thanks."

It happened again last night. My wife and I were eating at a local restaurant when I noticed in the next booth an old friend whom I had not seen for many years. I called to him, and he came over to our table. After a few minutes of interaction, I told him what I thought: "Floyd, I am reminded of what a good mind you have, and I will never forget what a great heart you have." I meant every word of it, and he knew it. And he beamed! I was expressing my appreciation for his gifts, which I had enjoyed through the years. My affirmation had a powerful effect on him.

The apostle Paul encourages us to see the positive and then to respond to God with thanksgiving. When you do, you make an investment in your own contentment, you enrich yourself down deep in your soul, and you maximize every relationship you have.

❀

Always give thanks for everything to our God and
Father in the name of our Lord Jesus Christ.

EPHESIANS 5:20

10

❦

Fully Obey the Truth
You Have

AFTER MORE THAN thirty years of working with people in psychotherapy, I have concluded that the decisions people make determine the quality of their life. It never fails: People who make good decisions have good lives, and people who make poor decisions have difficult lives.

Cliff Penner, my partner for the last twenty-eight years, is a great decision maker. He married the right woman, chose the right career, purchased the right house, selected the right church, gathered the right friends, and raised his children wisely. In fact, I asked him the other day if he would change anything if he could do it all over again. He thought for a while and then said, "I can't think of anything, so I guess not."

So the question is simply this: What makes Cliff Penner such a great decision maker?

One of the things that he does is to collect a lot of data for every decision. This data comes from three primary places: (1) what he thinks and feels about anything he must decide; (2) what the important people in his life think and feel about the decision he needs to make; and (3) what the important principles are that relate to the decision he must make. We call these principles values.

Cliff doesn't always take a long time to make a decision. I've watched him make thousands of them, and he's not obsessive about decision making. But he invariably refuses to make a choice until he is convinced that it lines up squarely with the "truth" as he knows it.

If someone wants him to deliver a speech on the other side of town, he gets *all* the information. He identifies his feelings about speaking at the particular time they want him. He checks with his wife, Joyce, with whom he almost always lectures. He considers the program in which he is being invited to participate. He estimates its value to the persons involved. Finally, when he has all the data collected, he weighs it all and makes a decision that is "obedient to the truth he has." Mind you, he is almost never wrong!

When you "fully obey the truth you have," the decision you make nearly always works out extremely well. So if your question is a little one like whether you should get up early tomorrow morning or not, or if it is a huge one like whether you should marry a particular person, the process always remains the same.

But the most critical part of this process is making sure that you *fully obey* the truth you have. You will be delightfully pleased with every decision you make that is in full obedience to this truth.

> *I hope all of you who are mature Christians*
> *will see eye-to-eye with me on these things,*
> *and if you disagree on some point, I believe that*
> *God will make it plain to you—if you*
> *fully obey the truth you have.*

PHILIPPIANS 3:15–16

11

※

Forget the Past and Look Forward to What Lies Ahead

I STOOD IN FRONT of the entire student body at the college I attended and made a total fool of myself.

As vice president of the freshman class, I had prepared a challenge to the sophomore class in relation to something called Rivalry Day.

"We all know that the freshman class is far superior to the sophomore class," I said. "And to prove it, we invite any sophomores brave enough to join us for an afternoon of contests requiring skill, strength, and clever thinking. Given these requirements, it's clear that freshmen have a distinct advantage, but sophomores can come and participate anyway. . . ."

On and on my blustery challenge went, delivered with all the forcefulness and intensity I could muster and read to a thousand people from a piece of paper I held in my hands:

One problem: I never imagined that my hands would shake at such a moment. But they did—and they shook so obviously that the incongruence between the bravado of my message and the pitifulness of my presentation was excruciatingly embarrassing. Like most embarrassing moments, it became even more painful the more I thought about it. So humiliated was I that attending class or walking across campus became a major ordeal.

Do you have things in your past that are embarrassing, or guilt-producing, or sickening, or frightening, or confusing? If you do, the goal is to work through them—AND FORGET THEM! It does absolutely no good to keep reminding yourself of those things in the past that caused you so much pain.

The secret to getting free from the past is to experience forgiveness. We may need the forgiveness of God, but we may also need the forgiveness of someone else—perhaps even our own forgiveness. The fact is that we need to be forgiven so we can point to the future—then we press on ahead. We focus our attention on what is *before* us, and we mobilize all our energy to deal with the challenges we face. When we do this, we maximize the likelihood that we will be successful.

Forget what is behind you that caused you pain. Focus on what is in front of you that looms as a worthy challenge for your attention. Summon all of your strength and energy to manage those future challenges triumphantly.

*No, dear brothers, I am still not all
I should be but I am bringing all my energies
to bear on this one thing: Forgetting the past and
looking forward to what lies ahead, I strain
to reach the end of the race.*

PHILIPPIANS 3:13–14

12

Quit Trying to Please People, and Focus on Pleasing God Alone

THE MOST IMPORTANT insight I've gained while working with people in the intimate relationship of psychotherapy is this: Most of us have a natural inclination to try to please the important people in our lives. Unfortunately, whether we please them or not, the result of this fixation never produces the deep-down contentment we so desperately seek.

I have often thought that the real tragedy of life is that we are born so small to people who are so large. In our tiny, helpless state, it is inevitable that these "big people" will become our masters. Obviously, there is nothing wrong with this in the beginning. When the tendency to please people becomes routine and habituated, however, it robs us of the liberating inner quality we call authenticity—that is, becoming the persons we truly are and summoning the courage to make decisions that demonstrate self-respect, self-regard, and self-honor. Sometimes this means making choices that go against the wishes and desires of others.

❧

The apostle Paul was brilliant in his own discovery of authenticity. He recognized his need to serve God rather than other people—even when they had the power to imprison him and rob him of freedom. He knew that his authenticity was far more important to his eventual contentment than any reward these persons could have provided—even if he totally satisfied their needs and desires.

Moreover, Paul's example removes all the anxiety that comes from dealing with persons who barter their approval of us on the basis of how well we satisfy their wishes. What he knows is that they are likely to give us only *conditional* love, the kind that comes with strings attached.

On the other hand, the unconditional love we so desperately need if we are to become authentic comes only from God. Interestingly enough, it is when we let God love us unconditionally at a deep level that we tend to become the person He really wants us to be. It is only when we feel His total love for us that we are free to be genuine in all of our relations with others. This genuineness, I feel confident, is exactly what pleases Him most.

Show me a person who is focused on pleasing God, and I will show you a person who is managing the vexing problems of life in a consistently masterful way.

You can see that I am not trying
to please you by sweet talk and flattery; no,
I am trying to please God.

GALATIANS 1:10

13

Look Forward to the Joys of Heaven

A MAN CAME to my office the other day with a severe marital problem. His wife had decided to leave him, and he was desperately anxious and depressed.

"I have to be honest," he said. "I wonder if life is worth living. I ask myself, *Why keep on living? What's the point of going on?*"

"That's a perfectly normal reaction in the midst of a painful ordeal like the one you're going through," I told him. "It can be tough to see beyond the current distress and anguish."

"I hear you, Doc," he replied slowly, "but I have to admit, I'm not just speaking hypothetically. I really don't know if I can go on."

I asked him some questions, and it became clear that he had seriously considered suicide. He was convinced that if his wife was not a part of his life, his existence was bound to be empty and dreary. He could not conceive of any kind of life he might develop on his own. Even more important, it never crossed his mind that he would ever experience anything beyond this life. In the midst of his devastating crisis, he could not see beyond the here and now.

One of the remarkable consequences of trusting in God is the recognition that "this moment" is only a speck on the huge mural that represents time and eternity. If this moment is terribly painful, you can be assured that it will soon be over, that time will be "swallowed up" in eternity.

Heaven is portrayed in all of Scripture as a place where God's immediate presence is most fully manifested, where the angels are, and where the redeemed shall ultimately be. It is represented as the place that does not have time boundaries, a place where every painful difficulty in this world will be dissolved.

The fact is, when we develop an intimate relationship with God, we become identified with Him both now and forever. As Martin Luther liked to say, "We take on all the virtues of Christ, and He takes on His back all of our defects and deficiencies." This is the miracle of that biblical principle called atonement. We become AT-ONE with God, and miraculously, He becomes AT-ONE with us.

As I have been able to communicate with my clients through the years, I am thankful to say that not a single one of the thousands of persons I have treated has committed suicide. Many of them have thought of it, some have threatened it, but no one has completed the act.

There is something so hopeful about "looking forward

to the joys of heaven." This perspective on the future makes the pain of the present so much more endurable.

And so, I told my client that while I understood the desperation of his current dilemma, I was confident that there is a continuation of life—beyond sadness, even beyond death—when we become at one with God through Christ. I assured him he could look forward to overcoming, to moving beyond the awfulness of his separation, and being home again.

These are joys that we must not miss! If we fail to incorporate this concept of heavenly joy in our consideration of life, we will have missed one of the most vital teachings of the Christian faith. With it, everything else becomes manageable. Look forward to the joys of heaven.

And you are looking forward to the joys
of heaven, and have been ever since the
Gospel first was preached to you.

COLOSSIANS 1:5

14

❧

Do Away with Sinful,
Earthly Things

I HAVE SPENT much of my career thinking about the matter of temptation—analyzing what it's all about and how to master it.

Temptation usually has to do with the allure of short-cuts in our lives, the appeal of doing something easy in hopes of achieving some sought-after goal. Since this approach almost never works, and since we pay a big price for taking the easy way out, these temptations should be avoided at all cost.

For instance, consider the issue of drinking alcohol. It isn't difficult to convince oneself that a drink or two will create such a soothing, mellow, relaxed state that whatever side effects may result would be well worth it. Usually, however, the mellow feeling lasts for only a few minutes, and the side effects have a more prolonged consequence. When drinking prompts more drinking and the cycle causes a person to become a problem drinker, the temptation has turned into tragedy. So much tragedy occurs when alcohol is abused that every effort should be made to help individuals avoid becoming addicted to it.

Alcohol is one of many shortcuts humans take, and all of them seem tempting at times. At one moment, a sexual affair may appear to offer the love we seek, gambling may seem a possible way out of our economic dilemma, cheating on taxes may strike us as a simple way to ease our "cash crunch," and bingeing on junk food may seem like an appropriate reward for our stressful day. These circumventions are popular because of our inability to recognize the difference between short-term gains and long-term losses.

If we want to live a good, fulfilling life, we will learn to master temptations. They almost always create far more pain than they are worth. Unfortunately, because they anesthetize our consciousness, we often overlook the pain they cause until a powerful addiction is formed.

The apostle Paul instructs us to do away with these destructive shortcuts, to mobilize our willpower against them. He has given us all the secrets for tapping into a power that enables us to manage the allure of unproductive things in our lives.

Away then with sinful, earthly things.

COLOSSIANS 3:5

15

Save Yourself a Lot of Trouble—
Refuse to Be a Hypocrite

I'VE LISTENED TO a lot of people through the years discussing the way they present themselves to friends and family. I have become convinced that telling and behaving truthfully is healthier and more beneficial in the long run than conveying any kind of pretense or falsehood.

I recall the story of a piano manufacturer who tried to get a testimonial from Will Rogers for his pianos. Rogers, who never endorsed any product unless he totally believed in it, wrote this letter to the piano firm: "Dear Sirs: I guess your pianos are the best I ever leaned against. Yours truly, Will Rogers."

Refusing to be a phony, under any circumstances, may cost you for a few moments, but the long-term effect is enormously positive.

There is something magnificently "unhypocritical" about little children. They tell the plain, unvarnished truth! In fact, I imagine you have encountered situations like this one:

"How do you do, my dear?" said the elderly lady to the little girl.

"Quite well, thank you," was the quiet reply.

There was a pause and then the lady asked, "Why don't you ask me how I am?"

"Because," said the child calmly, "I'm not interested."

If we could learn to shun hypocrisy like it was the plague, we would save ourselves an enormous amount of trouble. This is the case for two reasons.

First, our deep-down contentment as persons depends upon our being who we *truly* are. We are never more satisfied with our lives and ourselves than when we are honestly and completely the person God created us to be. I have involved myself in the lives of thousands of persons, and I have never found this principle to be wrong. When you become authentic, you move like a missile in the direction of internal meaning and satisfaction.

Second, hypocrisy, where it exists, violates and devastates relationships. When other people recognize that we present ourselves in false ways—ways designed to bolster our image or achieve some desired result—they lose confidence in us. Lost confidence produces defensiveness. Defensiveness keeps our interactions superficial and blocks intimacy. When this happens, our relationships fail to forge the kind of deep bond that is necessary to be fulfilling and meaningful.

The apostle Paul could never be accused of hypocrisy. He went right to the heart of the matter, and he presented himself with precision and forthrightness. As a matter of fact, on several occasions he jeopardized his very safety because of his refusal to shilly-shally or sidestep the truth. Throughout history, men and women who became well known for their lack of hypocrisy were the leaders who became most admired and most influential.

Shun hypocrisy! If you do, your relationships will be intense and enduring. You will inspire in every person you know the kind of trust and respect that always produces lifelong and satisfying friendships.

But when Peter came to Antioch I had to oppose him publicly, speaking strongly against what he was doing for it was very wrong.

GALATIANS 2:11

16

Don't Quarrel—Be Friends

FEW THINGS IN LIFE compare with the value of friendship. It is no surprise, therefore, that the hymn "What a Friend We Have in Jesus" is the most popular gospel song of all time.

I remember reading a quote from Alfred Adler a long time ago: "It is the individual who is not interested in his fellowmen who has the greatest difficulties in life and provides the greatest injury to others. It is among such individuals that all human failures spring." When you take no interest in others, when you have no friends, you are indeed poverty-stricken whether you know it or not.

When I was in graduate school at the University of Chicago in the late 1960s, I developed a big interest in the Chicago Bears football team. They had some of the greatest players I had ever watched, and the greatest of them was a running back named Gayle Sayers. In addition to his incredible power, he moved down the field with the grace and style of a dancer. His prowess was as much artistry as it was athleticism.

It was a time of great racial unrest in Chicago, and Sayers, a black man, had never had a close relationship with any white man before he met Brian Piccolo, a fullback for the Bears.

These two great athletes became friends over time and grew exceptionally close. Their relationship deepened into one of the most memorable friendships in the history of sports. As the movie *Brian's Song* poignantly depicts, the men truly loved each other.

Then tragedy occurred. During the 1969 season, Piccolo was diagnosed with cancer. He fought to play out that season, but he was in the hospital more than he was on the playing field. Throughout the battle with this terminal illness and in the middle of Piccolo's depression, these two athletes shared a special relationship. Sayers was constantly at the bedside of his friend, as the cancer tightened its grip on Piccolo's weakened body. Both men refused to surrender to it.

Sayers and Piccolo, along with their wives, had made plans to sit together at the annual Professional Football Writers Banquet in New York, and it was at this ceremony that Sayers was to receive the coveted George S. Halas award as "The most courageous player in professional football." But when it came time for the banquet, Piccolo was too sick to attend.

Anyone acquainted with those events will never forget

that when Sayers stood to receive his award, with the room filled with admiration and applause, he struggled to speak while choking back tears. He said: "You flatter me by giving me this award, but I tell you here and now that I accept this award not for me, but for Brian Piccolo. However, Brian cannot be here tonight. He is too ill. But Brian is a man who has more courage than any of us here tonight. I love Brian Piccolo, and I'd like you to love him, too. When you hit your knees tonight, please ask God to love him."

It wasn't long after that memorable night that Brian Piccolo died.

But these two powerful, tough football players had forged a friendship that allowed a true and caring love to develop between them. Their friendship had an enormous effect on millions of Americans just as it had on me.

It was Aristotle who said: "The antidote for fifty enemies is one friend." So whatever else you take away from this book, at least take this: Listen to your friends carefully and patiently, quarrel with them only after striving to understand them clearly, love them through good times and bad, and regard them as a great treasure. Surround yourself with a few true friends, and you will be rich beyond any measure.

Quarrel no more—be friends.

PHILIPPIANS 4:2

43

17

Deal with Your
Anger Immediately

RALPH WALDO EMERSON said, "For every minute you remain angry, you give up sixty seconds of peace of mind." If you enjoy inner peace and serenity more than you enjoy turmoil and tension, deal with your anger quickly.

Anger management has occupied my attention for years. I have experienced more than my own share of anger, have read thousands of pages of research and theory about it, have written a book about it, and have spoken hundreds of times on it across the country. Let me share with you three conclusions I've drawn from all of this thought and research.

First, no human emotion has so much potential for destructiveness—and constructiveness—as anger. When your body experiences such a surge of adrenaline and energy, you are going to do something powerful—either for good or for bad. Because of this, you should have great respect for this emotion. When you become angry, you need to know how to stay in control of yourself. You must become an expert at dealing with this emotion in your life.

Second, in order to become an expert, you have to work hard at it when you are *not* angry. You need to understand that anger is always produced in response to hurt, frustration, and fear. Moreover, you need to recognize that the goal of anger is to reduce this primary pain in your life, to make it unnecessary for you to have to reexperience the discomfort that produced the anger in the first place.

If you will become an expert in managing your anger, you can do tremendous things. In the Bible, God is portrayed as the angriest person of all. There are 455 uses of the word *anger* in the Old Testament, and 375 of them refer to God's anger. In the New Testament, Jesus is frequently angry. Scripture tells us that before some of His greatest miracles, He was filled with indignation. If you can become as good at expressing your anger as God or Jesus, as well as the prophets and the great church leaders, you will be able to channel the power toward positive, productive ends.

Third, the more quickly you deal with your anger toward someone else, the better. The apostle Paul says, "Don't let the sun go down on your anger." In essence, he says, "Deal with it *now!*"

What Paul is saying is that anger has a way of becoming acidic to your inner self and to any relationship it affects. Thus, you want to utilize this "physiological pre-paredness" *immediately* to deal therapeutically with the hurt, frustration, or fear. If you don't, you risk damaging your relationships with the anger.

If you manage it quickly and sensibly, you will discover that your anger can promote a successful resolution of your conflict, which will result in a richer relationship. Deal with anger *early,* skillfully, and respectfully! You will be amazed at how effectively you can turn a difficult moment into one of meaning and fulfillment.

If you are angry . . . get over it quickly.

EPHESIANS 4:26

18

Let Your Hearts
Be Flooded with Light

I HAVE HAD hundreds of people come to me for psychotherapy whose heads enjoyed far more light than their hearts.

What I mean is, they could *think* better than they could feel, "cognize" better than they could experience.

When it came to their spiritual faith, then, these men and women knew most of what was important about Christianity. Unfortunately, many of them didn't actually *feel* very loved, forgiven, or cherished. They had very little "light" in their hearts.

I will never forget the prominent minister who came to me many years ago suffering from depression. After his physician performed a careful physical examination, it was determined that his depression was not a result of anything biochemical. Its impetus had to do with how he felt about himself. This man, in his mid-fifties, knew as much or more than I did about the love of God. He could talk about it at great length, quote many verses about it, and he had preached scores of sermons on the topic.

"It sounds to me like you *know* everything about God's love," I told him. "But let me ask you this: Do you *feel* loved by God?"

He thought for a long time, and then said, "No, I don't. I tell all my parishioners how much God loves them, how He accepts them unconditionally, but deep down I don't feel worthy of God's love."

Because he felt unlovable at his core, this pastor's life was gray unto black. Moreover, he had surrounded himself with people who reinforced his way of thinking and behaving—people who said and did all the right things, but who had apparently never had a true encounter with God's love and grace. These people knew the gospel perfectly well in their heads and practiced it with precision—but they didn't *experience* it in their hearts.

It became obvious to me that this man was going to have to break out of his experiential darkness—into the light that would allow him to feel deeply within his heart. He had to *experience* the gospel at the deepest of levels—not just rationally, but personally as well. It needed to become as real to him as if God had physically hugged him and held him in His arms for a long period of time.

And as we worked together for several months, I did everything in my power to help him achieve a new and intimate relationship with this God who has such tremendous love for him. As he began to sense that it was true, everything about his life took on a totally different perspective.

One of the things that he began to sense was the incredible future he had—a future that extended into the far reaches of eternity. As he became more deeply aware of how much God loves him, he took on a whole new appreciation of the magnificent life he had been given. I am happy to say that his depression lifted and the blackness vanished. They were replaced by hope and light.

It can be that way for all people when their hearts are flooded with the light that comes from Love—a love that is just for them.

I pray that your hearts will be flooded with light.

Ephesians 1:18

19

Break Free
from Evil Desires

"I'm engaged to be married to a good woman," my client told me, "but I crave sex with a lot of different women, and my fiancée says she won't put up with my craziness anymore!"

This man—thirty-seven years old, six feet tall, handsome, and dressed in natty clothes—told me in lurid detail how he spent his free hours searching for women. He had purchased an expensive car, and he cruised the beach communities and the Hollywood streets looking for women with whom he might have a few minutes of sexual pleasure.

He suffered from a severe sexual addiction, and both his career and his personal life were filled with chaos because he was a slave to his perverted passion. Every day! Every hour! He wanted the same thing again and again. He was a prisoner of his sickness. He didn't have the faintest idea of how to be freed from his hell on earth.

❦

The apostle Paul says, in essence, "When you come to Christ, He sets you free from your evil desires." He says, "You die, as it were, with Christ and this sets you free from following the world's ideas of how to be saved" (see Colossians 2:11–12).

Admittedly, gaining freedom isn't easy. The pattern my client had developed required intensive therapy, strict accountability, and constant interaction with a person who could help him appropriate the Holy Spirit's power and strength. When an addiction is so deeply ingrained, it requires in-hospital treatment. And that's what I got for this man—immediately!

But the intensive treatment he required had to be grounded in the person and power of Christ. After all, when you have Christ in you, you are literally "filled up" with God Himself. And Paul says that Christ is the highest Ruler, with authority over every other power (Colossians 1:16). No addiction can ultimately resist the power of Christ when His power rules at the center of your life.

You will be set free! It may not occur in a single moment. It may require a relational process with one of Christ's chosen workers. But your freedom is guaranteed. No problem—no matter how deeply rooted—can prevail over the power you receive when Christ enters your life.

When you came to Christ
he set you free from your evil desires.

COLOSSIANS 2:11

20

Throw Off Your Old
Evil Nature

WHEN YOU LOOK closely at yourself, do you see some stubborn, obstinate traits you once thought you had conquered? When I look at myself, I know I do.

For instance, I periodically recognize how competitive I am. I seem to think, at times, that if someone does better than I do that I can't be a winner. In fact, I sometimes fear that to have someone outcompete me means that I am a loser.

So when I don't catch myself, I travel too fast on the highway to make sure that I stay ahead of traffic—or at least stay even with others. Sometimes I brag about my kids' virtues in an unnecessary effort to compete with someone else's kids, I find myself wanting to buy a car that will raise my status above that of others, and I have a hard time praising others for qualities that are greater than my own.

I catch myself being selfish, lustful, impatient, unkind,

and prideful. Do you ever find any of these characteristics in yourself? I suppose we will never totally get rid of some of these qualities . . . but we can if we want to and we try.

You see, every one of these qualities comes from our unwillingness to let Christ's love dominate us to the very center of our beings. If we let Him love us the way He wants to, we are suddenly released from our need to compete, exaggerate, criticize, boast, and show off. We're lovable!

And therein lies the secret of throwing off our old evil nature. We don't need to be our own god. The one true God is not only willing to do the job, but He's the only one who *can* do it.

Let Christ dominate your life with His love, and then get about the task of throwing off the rotten old evil nature that used to be so much a part of the ineffective, awkward, and unattractive person you once were.

> *Then throw off your old evil nature—the old you*
> *that was a partner in your evil ways—rotten*
> *through and through, full of lust and sham.*
>
> EPHESIANS 4:22

21

Stop Being Mean,
Bad Tempered, and Angry

I'll call him Mr. Jones, but his real name is imprinted on my brain for life. Every student at my high school feared Mr. Jones, who was a physical education instructor. He was the meanest, worst-tempered, and angriest person I have ever met.

One day at lunchtime, two friends and I were peeping through a keyhole of the equipment room to see the new jerseys our basketball team was going to receive later that day. We were taking turns excitedly looking at the uniforms when all of a sudden I received a mighty kick to my rear end from old Mr. Jones. *Ouch!*

He assumed that we were up to no good, and he used physical force to express his point. "Get out of here!" he yelled.

I remember feeling so misunderstood, so unfairly attacked. His hateful act, so filled with venom, served as a profound lesson to me through the years. For Mr. Jones clearly was an unhappy, miserable man. If all of us thought he was mean to students during the school day, it must have been horrible for anyone having to *live* with him. Think what it must have been like for this grouch to live with *himself* all the time.

When you encounter someone like Mr. Jones, when you struggle to maintain your patience and composure in the midst of harsh treatment, don't forget to recognize the underlying cause of all that hostility. Sour people have undoubtedly received little love, and they have never learned to deliver much to themselves—or to anyone else. Their hearts are hard because love has not been allowed to perform its softening magic.

What a transformation old Mr. Jones could have undergone had he encountered the powerful love of God. What a different man he would have been for all of us, for those related to him, and most of all for himself.

Meanness, ill temper, and vengeful anger have such a vicious effect on everybody—but especially on the one who experiences it and spreads it to others.

Stop being mean, bad-tempered and angry.
Quarreling, harsh words, and dislike of others
should have no place in your lives.

EPHESIANS 4:31

22

Be Full of Joy

THINK ABOUT A time when you experienced great pleasure or delight. What exactly did you feel? What evoked that feeling in you? How long did it last? What would you give to have an experience like that again?

Joy is the emotion we have when we feel safe, secure, hopeful, and energized. It is what we experience when we're confident that our good fortune will continue over time. It is a feeling of bliss. We can hardly keep from laughing out loud!

It is this kind of joy that can characterize your life.

Now I want you to think of that person in your life whom you would name as the most joyful person you know. Can you see in your mind's eye? Think about what it is in this individual's life that contributes to his or her joyfulness. How can that person maintain a sense of rejoicing moment by moment, day by day?

It's likely that the joyful person you thought of has discovered what the apostle Paul discovered. He says we should be full of joy all the time—because all the big issues in our lives have been taken care of. We are loved to our core. We know without a doubt that we could never be loved any more or any less, no matter what we do. If we trust God, if we know deep in our hearts that He is in charge of our lives, we can get about the exciting task of discovering who we really are and being that person genuinely.

As we do this, we are encouraged to delight in the life God has given us, to have good humor, to be glad and merry, to live fully every day we have on earth.

How good it is to be reminded that we need not be so serious, so glum, so constantly focused on achievement. How wonderful to know we are free to laugh, to cackle, to see the funny side—and most of all to celebrate that we are able, with God's help, to manage any challenge in our life.

Take full advantage of the wonderful opportunity to enjoy yourself and your life!

Always be full of joy in the Lord;
I say it again, rejoice!

PHILIPPIANS 4:4

23

Distinguish Clearly
Right from Wrong

ONE OF THE best things that ever happened to me didn't strike me as very good at the time.

I was a fifth grader, and my schoolmate Rodney Lee and I were in a grocery store. I was a naive kid, and he seemed "worldly-wise." We were hungry as we walked the aisles of that store, and before long we came to the bakery section.

Rodney pulled me aside and whispered, "Hey, Neil, you see that Boston cream pie over there?"

"Yeah, sure," I said hesitantly, knowing what might be coming next.

"When I give you the all clear sign, take the pie and tuck it inside your coat. Then I'll walk out of the store and you follow behind me." He saw my wary look, so he added, "C'mon, it'll be a cinch!"

A few seconds later as we walked briskly toward the door, I heard the loudspeaker blare, "Will the two boys who are leaving the store come upstairs immediately!" A dozen clerks and shoppers were staring at us, and I knew we had no escape.

Every part of my body trembled as we ascended the stairs and entered a glass-enclosed area that overlooked the store. A man who looked like a giant to me met us there and took us to a small room. I will never forget what he said: "Who do you want me to call—the juvenile officers or your parents?"

These two alternatives were equally horrifying to my ten-year-old brain. So I began to chatter, "Please, sir, don't call either one of them. I promise you this, if you won't call anyone, I'll never, ever do such an awful thing again." My voice was shaking so badly that I had a hard time getting the words out.

Wisely, the man let us "blow in the breeze" for a while. The longer he waited, the more committed I became to leaving behind my life of crime forever. He finally let us go with a long lecture.

It was a profound lesson for me, one that I am delighted I learned at such a young age. For when the line between right and wrong is allowed to blur, character deterioration, a corrosive human and societal experience, is almost always the consequence. All of this can be prevented if we keep the boundaries between right and wrong as clear as possible. The manager of that grocery store certainly did his part! Without knowing it, he undoubtedly did me an enormous favor.

❧

*For I want you always to see clearly the difference
between right and wrong, and to be inwardly clean,
no one being able to criticize you from now
until our Lord returns.*

PHILIPPIANS 1:10

24

Always Be Generous
and Unselfish

NO ONE CARES to be around selfish people much. But have you ever stopped to ask yourself *why* selfish people are that way? I have found that there are two primary reasons why people turn out to be self-seeking and self-serving.

First, these individuals have spent too many moments feeling deprived of enough love to meet their needs, and this lack often produces someone who is excessively self-absorbed, who concentrates on his own advantage, pleasure, or well-being without regard for others.

Second, some selfish persons have been shown *too much* attention and have learned to share too little with others. They also end up self-absorbed and unable to empathize with others' needs.

I once had a friend who fell into both of these categories. He was never taught to share and give to others, and therefore he had serious deficiencies when it came to generosity. He always waited for me to pay when a waitress would bring a check to our table. Sometimes he would offer to "pay his part," but "his part" always turned out to be significantly less than he really owed.

Over time I grew weary of his selfishness. People always grow weary of those who focus excessively on themselves, who seek their own advantage.

The apostle Paul makes it clear that when we transmit the same kind of generous love that God shows us to everyone around us, we experience a rich by-product—deep-down, soul-satisfying contentment.

To be unselfish, accept God's unconditional love and give away that love as fast as you receive it.

Don't be selfish.

PHILIPPIANS 2:3

25

Look for the Positive

MOANERS AND GROANERS are a pain to be around, don't you agree?

I know a married couple who always look for the negative in every situation. They work each other into a frenzy about some real or imagined problem, and complain to their friends about it. If anyone suggests an opposing opinion, they argue with high-pitched, whiny voices.

Any psychologist will tell you that people like this are the most difficult clients to have in therapy, because they present a dilemma: You can never satisfy them, but they'll never let you quit trying. You're trapped!

If *you* tend to be a person who focuses on the negative in other people or life events, and if you have a tendency to complain and criticize, I challenge you to alter your perspective. Look for the positive from now on.

I give you that admonition knowing for certain that chronic complaining will earn you a reputation of being peevish and unenjoyable. Other people will find a way to distance themselves from you, and you will have even more to complain about.

Make a concerted effort to be positive and cheerful and you will become a popular member of your church, neighborhood, workplace, and social network. You will be someone who contributes to the growth and cohesiveness of the people you associate with, and the deficiencies of everything around you will disappear as the rich qualities of others multiply in response to your reinforcement.

In everything you do,
stay away from complaining and arguing.

PHILIPPIANS 2:14

26

Savor Your Freedom

MY WIFE, MARYLYN, and I—along with our three daughters—lived in Switzerland for a year. We traveled a lot during that time, and we visited numerous countries. We saw the Alps, quaint villages, and pristine lakes, and we met dozens of wonderful European people.

When we returned to America and I had time to reflect on all that I had seen and done, I was struck by the sense of freedom I had here at home to go anywhere I wanted and to be the person I really wanted to be.

Freedom is an incredibly important context in which to become emotionally healthy. That's the genius of the Christian faith—it is based entirely on the liberating unconditional love God has for every person. The immediate result of this powerful love is that all persons are set free from the entanglements that have ensnared them throughout their lives.

The kind of love God offers us—free of any stipulations

or prerequisites—is far different from that of our earthly relationships. From the time we're infants, we learn to respond to the criteria placed on us by other people in order to receive their love. No human being loves us unconditionally as God does, and most people require something of us in order to share their love with us.

So we frantically try to satisfy the criteria people require of us—if we want their affirmation. For instance, my dad wanted me to be a strong, aggressive person, so around him I denied the more tender parts of myself. My mother, on the other hand, wanted me to be gentle and soft, with no anger or assertiveness, and similarly, I denied facets of my personality when I was around her.

When we barter away our authenticity by trying to meet everybody else's needs for us, we become slaves to *inauthenticity*. That's why God's unconditional love for us is so crucial. It sets us free from all these old entanglements that have kept us from becoming the persons we were created to be. What a phenomenal gift this freedom is! All of a sudden, we have only one real goal and challenge in our lives—to be who we were created to be.

While we can listen to what the important people want from us, and while we search for the wisdom that comes from holding sound values, we continually make choices about who we will be in each moment. These choices are likely to be great choices, because we are free.

How can we savor such freedom? Because the biggest question of all has been answered for all time. That question is: How can I become lovable? My "lovability" has been established once and for all because of what God did for me.

Freedom! We must never give anyone the right to take it away from us. It is a treasure more valuable than any other.

Christ has made us free.

GALATIANS 5:1

27

Have Nothing to Do
with Sexual Sin

SEXUAL SIN AND adulterous affairs almost always sink a marriage. The resulting distrust corrodes so many parts of the marriage that it spreads like a cancer.

Why is this so? Because sexuality involves the deepest form of intimacy, sharing that is so private it cannot adequately be put into words. Intimacy is sacred between two people. If you violate this intimacy, the person who has entrusted his or her deepest feelings and thoughts to you will no longer feel that you are trustworthy.

That's why the apostle Paul says without equivocation, "Have nothing to do with sexual sin, impurity, lust and shameful desires."

As a psychologist, I have counseled dozens of husbands and wives whose marriages were severely damaged by various sexual sins. Often these marriages can be saved, but it requires a thorough rebuilding of the broken trust between the two people and an enormous commitment.

This rebuilding requires careful guidance by a highly capable psychologist, and there will almost always be crying and excruciatingly painful feelings.

I say to every new couple I work with: "Mobilize your willpower to maintain sexual fidelity in your marriage! Whatever else you do, be trustworthy in this area. Have nothing to do with sexual sin. If you will steer clear of every kind of sexual impropriety, you will do more than protect your marriage—you will protect your own soul. For if you violate someone else, you will violate yourself as well." Great marital relationships are solidly based in sexual fidelity.

Away then with sinful, earthly things;
deaden the evil desires lurking within you;
have nothing to do with sexual sin, impurity,
lust and shameful desires.

COLOSSIANS 3:5

28

Watch Out If You Are Always Critical and Catty

HAVE YOU EVER been stabbed in the back by someone intent on doing you in, bringing you down, ruining your reputation? What a painful experience!

If you find yourself going after other people in a sarcastic and critical way, take a long look at your own life. The New Testament warns us in a highly specific way to stop belittling and disparaging others because it leads to hurt, anger, and division.

Sarcasm, what Paul refers to as "cattyness," is a form of underhanded anger expression. People who underhandedly express their anger try to score put-down points without taking responsibility for their actions. This kind of anger mismanagement is sometimes difficult to catch, but when you look for it—in yourself or in others—you quickly become aware of its devastating power and its consistently negative results.

If you realize that you are occasionally or regularly critical and catty, take a thorough inventory of your internal world. Check to see how deeply loved you have allowed yourself to be, how right your relationship with God is. Search to see if there are unresolved hurts that may be causing your anger to spill out onto others. If this is the case, take whatever action is necessary to ensure healing.

For instance, see if there is a pattern to your criticism. If you find yourself thinking that other people are "show-offs" and "desperate for attention," see if that might be one of your own issues. Or if you are hostile toward people who don't remember you even after they have been introduced to you several times, check yourself for the same problem. I frequently find that I criticize people for what I find most frustrating about myself.

Only after a careful internal inventory should you criticize the other person, the target of your barbed remarks. It may be that the individual has deficiencies that need to be addressed. If so, proceed only if your motivations are right—to help, support, and encourage—and keep your discussion positive. Remember that we're all in this game of life together. We are trying the best we know how to become healthy individuals, friends, and partners.

> *But if instead of showing love among yourselves*
> *you are always critical and catty, watch out!*
> *Beware of ruining each other.*
>
> GALATIANS 5:15

29

Pay Attention to God During Good Times and Bad

WHEN THINGS ARE going well for us, it's sometimes easy to ignore God. We forget to read His Word, and we lose our enthusiasm for praying to Him. If this happens to us, we are vulnerable to enormous difficulty.

After I spoke at a local church one recent Sunday, an attractive middle-aged couple approached me to talk. The man stood quietly, showing great interest, while his wife told me in a concise way a rather common story.

She said that some years earlier she had become seriously ill with a mysterious ailment. For five long years, she was paralyzed, unable to move any part of her body. Obviously, she required extensive medical care.

"During that terrible period," she said, "I prayed all the time. There was nothing else I could do. I guess you could say I became a prayer warrior. Because of all those hours talking with the Lord, I developed a very intense relationship with Him."

In time, her condition began to change, and she slowly returned to full health.

"And now my health is perfect again," she said. "As a matter of fact, I am enjoying some success as an artist."

"*Huge* success," her husband said.

"But here's my dilemma," she continued. "I find that days and even weeks go by when I don't talk to God. I am ashamed to say that my need for Him seems to be significantly less. I know that it really isn't, but I don't *feel* the need like I did before. Actually, I sometimes act like I can go it on my own now. What should I do?"

With a line of people waiting to speak with me, I took sixty seconds to tell her how strongly I believe that when things are going well, we should *double* the length of our devotional times. During those times when life is good, when we enjoy success and prosperity, we should greatly increase our efforts at maintaining a close relationship with the Lord. The fact is, when the seas of our life are calm, we become vulnerable to all kinds of temptations designed to eliminate God from our lives.

Pain is often a great teacher. It leads us directly to the throne of God. Good times, on the other hand, often do just the opposite—they lead us to believe we're self-sufficient, that we can be self-reliant. We must remain alert to our persistent need for God's involvement in our life. This involvement should include conscious effort and discipline on our part. When it does, it will take us to the reality of our neediness. It will lead us back to the loving arms of our Father—and that will change everything about our existence.

> *Don't be misled; remember that you can't ignore*
> *God and get away with it: a man will always*
> *reap just the kind of crop he sows!*

GALATIANS 6:7

30

Live Clean, Innocent Lives

ONE OF MY favorite Bible stories involves the mothers who brought their children to Jesus for a blessing.

> The disciples shooed them away, telling them not to bother him.
>
> But when Jesus saw what was happening he was very much displeased with his disciples and said to them, "Let the children come to me, for the Kingdom of God belongs to such as they. Don't send them away! I tell you as seriously as I know how that anyone who refuses to come to God as a little child will never be allowed into his Kingdom."
>
> Then he took the children into his arms and placed his hands on their heads and he blessed them. (Mark 10:13–16)

Our goal is to live clean, innocent lives as *children* of God. Think for a moment about what this means. First, we don't play mind games with other people—or even with ourselves. We see things honestly and clearly, and we are sincere and straightforward in our interactions with others.

Second, we don't try to take shortcuts in our lives. We meet challenges head-on, we confront problems, and we persevere through hard times to celebrate good times. We play life as it comes to us, and we refuse to manipulate it to our own ends.

Finally, we have ultimate trust and faith. We expect everything to be all right. We move ahead with full confidence in our expectation.

Obviously, the instruction to live clean lives also includes not lying, cheating, holding grudges, or violating the rights of others. When we avoid these actions, we are sure to experience contentment. When our days are lived with childlike innocence, honesty, and trust, we will be filled with the joy and gladness of God's blessing.

You are to live clean, innocent lives
as children of God in a dark world full of
people who are crooked and stubborn. Shine
out among them like beacon lights.

PHILIPPIANS 2:15

31

❧

Love God and Serve
His People

TRUE CHRISTIAN FAITH is contagious! When you are
loved by the one true God, the all-powerful God, it changes
everything about your existence. Your inspiration level
rises to the sky. You feel like helping other people and
serving them in every way you can.

The apostle Paul encourages us to spend almost no time
privately luxuriating in the joy that comes from being
loved by God. He says to us, "Now that you have been
saved and made glad, do everything in your power to
brighten the life of every person you meet."

The principle that giving love away increases our enjoyment of it is crucial for multiplying the abundance of our
lives. There are thousands of ways that we can give this
love away. We can hold the door open for someone who is
following us out of our office building. We can help push
someone out of a snowdrift. We can send a note to a discouraged person we know. We can call a friend who is

going through a tough time. We can congratulate persons we know who are enjoying success and achievement.

This is what the kingdom of God is all about—people loving each other. It all starts with getting yourself into a loving relationship with God, then getting about the task of caring for one another. Your marriage will become significantly better. Your friendships will grow even more meaningful. Your family relationships will take on more vitality. Your neighborhood organization will stimulate your best effort. And your church will have more importance to you than it's ever had before. It is a matter of people loving people because they have been loved at the depths of their being by a God who just keeps coming after them.

So if you're ever tempted to hoard the riches of your faith or privately bask in the joy of your Christian experience, consider a whole different approach. Use your freedom to help other people in every way you can.

Remember the double emphasis of the Christian life: Trust God and serve His people.

Dear brothers, you have been given freedom:
not freedom to do wrong, but freedom to
love and serve each other.

GALATIANS 5:13

32

Love Others as You
Love Yourself

IT IS A FASCINATING discovery of modern-day psychology that virtually everyone loves others to the same degree that they *truly* love themselves. When people care for others in a superficial and insensitive way, they inevitably have a shallow and inaccurate view of themselves.

The adequacy of a person's self-concept largely determines his level of emotional health. If he has never been set free to build a strong and durable self-concept, he becomes vulnerable to all the troublesome aspects of life. For instance, neuroses are always the result of an inadequately developed self-concept. Depression, phobias, and obsessiveness all get started as an effort to deal with the anxiety one experiences about one's perceived inability to respond to the challenges of life.

Interestingly, developing a solid self-concept is perfectly possible if you go about it the right way. You have to recognize that the "building materials" that go into a healthy self-concept are the choices you make from moment to moment. If these choices do not come from inside you but are made instead to satisfy, for example, others' expectations, they will not help you become the kind of strong, healthy person who loves himself in an accurate and sufficient way. You have to get freed up from the outside in order to turn your attention to the inside. It is inside that you make the choices that ultimately determine the person you are. This person is what your self-concept is all about. Get it right, and you will be on your way to loving yourself and others.

So, if you find yourself impatient with others, overly critical, unkind, unforgiving, and selfish, what you know is that you haven't been "saved" from your own impossible efforts to save yourself. Therefore, you get caught up in competing with others.

This negative possibility is at the root of Paul's encouragement to recognize the Law as a great teacher. For instance, he says that the whole Law can be summed up in one criterion: Love others as you love yourself. If you find yourself not loving others, you have broken the Law. And so, you must strive to discover how to keep the Law.

Do you love others? Do you love others as you love yourself? If so, you are undoubtedly in a right relationship with God! But if you find yourself focusing all of your attention on your own life exclusive of others, you can know for a fact that you haven't loved yourself the way you need to. All the love you need is totally available to you right now! God is ready to love you so powerfully that your love for others will become automatic and natural.

The bottom line is this: You can't save yourself by keeping the Law, but the Law can be a good teacher. Check yourself out, and see if you are loving others and loving yourself. If you are, celebrate! If you aren't, you know exactly what to do.

> *For the whole Law can be summed up in this one command: "Love others as you love yourself."*
>
> GALATIANS 5:14

33

Always Remember
to Help the Poor

My dad died a few years ago, and a number of people stepped forward at his funeral to tell stories about how he had made a difference in their lives. Of all the stories told that day, I loved one in particular.

"My name is Jack Dyer," said a tall, burly, rough-hewn man in his mid-fifties. "I want to tell you about the way Otis Warren helped me when I was down on my luck. I am a carpenter by trade, and we carpenters have good seasons and bad seasons. Sometimes we're busy and sometimes we aren't. During one of the bad seasons, I totally ran out of money. My wife and I and our three children had no food—I mean *no* food—and our bills were piled high.

"I thought to myself, *Who can I possibly go to for help?* My mind immediately settled on O. J. Warren. I went to his office and asked if I could borrow a hundred dollars. In the kindest of ways, he said he'd be happy to help."

Jack told how my father pulled out his checkbook and wrote the check. He put it in an envelope, jotted JACK DYER on the front, sealed it, and told him to take it to his bank for immediate cash.

"When I got to the bank," Jack continued, "I handed the envelope to the teller without even opening it. I waited for the money, and she began to count it out for me. But soon I knew she had made a mistake. She was giving me way too much. When I pointed out the error, she held up the check for me to see. I couldn't believe it—O. J. had written it for *three hundred* dollars. That's all I want to tell you about my friend Otis Warren."

My dad never talked about the times he gave to the poor—he wasn't one to boast or pat himself on the back—but he did tell me how he learned to be generous.

There was a time as a young man when he worked as a Chevrolet dealer, and he had no money at all. He went to his dad and told him he needed help. Without hesitation, his dad said, "Go down to the farm and tell your mother that you and I talked. Ask her to write out a check for everything we have in our savings account."

Then my dad would always tell me how much he appreciated his father's generosity and how often his dad would say, "Whatever I have is yours."

When Jack Dyer told that story about Otis Warren at the funeral, I knew my dad had continued the tradition of caring for the poor that was so crucial to the teaching of Jesus' disciples. Whatever else those first-century

Christians believed in, they never forgot the poor. They knew how much they had been given, and they shared with those less fortunate. We should be eager to do the same.

> *The only thing they did suggest*
> *was that we must always remember to help*
> *the poor, and I, too, was eager for that.*
>
> GALATIANS 2:10

34

Help a Brother Gain Release
from His "Sin Trap"

MILLIONS OF AMERICANS are ensnared in what the apostle Paul calls "sin traps." Some people don't even know they're trapped, while others know it all too well. From time to time, all of us get caught, and when we do, we desperately need another person's help to get free.

Some sin traps are obvious. Thousands of Americans drink too much alcohol and become addicted to it, and it has disastrous effects on their lives. They need our help.

Millions of Americans can't control their anger. They become trapped in their rage and fury. Some ten million children are beaten by their angry parents every year. Five to seven million American women are physically abused by their husbands each year. Verbal assaults on persons are a constant source of mind-destroying venom. These anger mismanagers may or may not recognize the trap they are in, but they need our help.

Other sin traps are much more subtle and difficult to

recognize. For instance, some persons desperately try to secure more status, to move to the top of the corporate ladder. They work night and day, and they become obsessed with "getting ahead" and earning the praise and admiration of those around them.

Other people are engaged in a sin trap that might be labeled anesthetization. They watch television seven or eight hours a day, play video games until their eyes blur, shop till they drop, or run on a perpetual treadmill of busyness, filling their lives with meaningless pursuits. They are a long way from "saving their souls," but they remain frozen in their lostness.

Everyone who is caught in a sin trap, whether they recognize it or not, desperately needs the help of those around them. When we help them, we set *ourselves* up to be helped the next time. You can be sure that all of us are going to end up in some kind of a sin trap at one point or another, and when we do, it will be a cause for celebration when somebody helps us get out of it.

Dear brothers, if a Christian is overcome
by some sin, you who are godly should gently
and humbly help him back onto the right path,
remembering that next time it might be
one of you who is in the wrong.

GALATIANS 6:1

35

Share Each Other's Troubles

I HAVE A highly valued friend named Sandy Shapero, who is a rabbi. I have seldom met a more delightful and caring person.

Sandy was the first person we called when my wife was going through a frightening physical illness a few years ago. He was CEO and president of the City of Hope, a prestigious hospital in the Los Angeles area. We asked for his help, and he gave us far more than help. Oh, he gave us useful advice and put us in touch with important physicians at his hospital. But he did a whole lot more than that—he became involved in our trouble, and he called us frequently from all over the United States as he traveled.

"Neil, I'm at a conference in New York," he would say, "but I wanted to call and see how you're doing."

A week later, we would get another call. "I'm off to a board of directors meeting, but before I go, I just had to phone and tell you I'm thinking about you."

Sandy's caring meant the world to us at a very difficult time in our lives.

Recently, Sandy has encountered some challenging times of his own. He has been involved in a power struggle with his former employer, and it's been an horrendous experience for him. Marylyn and I have supported and encouraged Sandy as best we know how. We have prayed passionately for him, and we have offered whatever expertise we have.

Throughout the struggles we have all experienced, I have been reminded how often the apostle Paul encourages us to get involved with *each other* when we are enduring difficult times. To have people wrap their loving, supportive arms around us makes all the difference in the world.

Share each other's troubles and problems,
and so obey our Lord's command. If anyone
thinks he is too great to stoop to this, he is
fooling himself. He is really a nobody.

GALATIANS 6:2–3

36

View Your Brothers and Sisters as Equals

WERE YOU BORN into a family of average economic means, or were you born into an unusually wealthy or unusually poor family? Were you born into an emotionally healthy family or one replete with problems and dysfunction? Were you born into a family that was part of the majority, or were your born into a minority family?

Sometimes these distinctions seem to mean so much. If we're not careful, we let these factors separate us from one another. The fact is, though, the only factor that *really* matters is whether or not we're members of God's family. The most important consideration in any person's life is where he or she stands in relation to the one true God.

If you and an individual of any color, economic means, nationality, or family background stand together in your response to God, you have *everything* in common. God sees you as equals in every way—fully loved, forgiven, and accepted. You are both children of the King and are given the same rich inheritance and place of honor. You are both called to a life of faith and caring for each other that is absolutely equal.

So if your brother is black and you are white, if your sister is rich and you are poor, if your friend is healthy and you are emotionally troubled—you have the same standing and status. You are in this together. That will mean everything when it comes to the way that you treat one another.

Ultimately, you will have all things in common. And once you recognize this, you will want to do everything in your power to help your sisters and brothers in every way you can.

We are all parts of one body,
we have the same Spirit, and we have all
been called to the same glorious future.

EPHESIANS 4:4

37

Be a New and
Different Person

DURING MY THIRTY-THREE years as a clinical psychologist, I have seen several thousand individuals and couples who were struggling to be "new and different persons." One in particular comes to mind—a woman I will refer to as Pat.

Pat was one of seven children born to an alcoholic father and a hardworking but emotionally fragile mother. Because Pat had poor vision that was uncorrected during her childhood, she developed a phobia about school. She came to think of herself as "stupid, dim-witted, and intellectually deficient." Her self-esteem was perilously low, and she became a "Ping-Pong ball" for the neighborhood children and her brothers and sisters, who used her in whatever way they wished.

Pat was given little attention by her parents. Her father came home drunk every night. Pat's mother tried to provide stability for the family, but her emotional reserves were so depleted that she allowed horrible things to happen within the family. Pat, for instance, nearly died on one occasion from a long illness that her mother neglected, and to say that Pat was given insufficient love and security is a great understatement.

Pat grew to be physically beautiful, and she gained some leverage in life through her beauty. She married a good-hearted but troubled man, and in time she had a child and began to earn a living. Through all of this, though, her inner self was broken and her soul withered.

When she came to see me in psychotherapy, I tried as hard as I knew how to help her encounter the unconditional love of God in a personal and consistent way. Initially, her life involved one crisis after another, and chaotic events were almost daily occurrences. But God's love kept pursuing Pat in her desperate times—as well as her infrequent happy ones. She couldn't get out of the way of this all-encompassing love.

Eventually her life began to change from the inside out. God's message—that she had tremendous value and worth—kept coming at her, and the only requirement was that she believe and trust in Jesus.

Her experience of being loved took root, and everything about her life slowly became new and different. She let go of her pessimism and became optimistic and hopeful about her future. She began looking at others in light of their attributes, and her criticism and hostility vanished.

She recognized her incredible potential for growth, and she developed career goals.

Pat studied to earn her high school diploma, enrolled in a junior college and finished that program in two years, and graduated at the top of her class from a university. Now she is about to finish a doctoral degree.

More important than those academic achievements are the changes in her sense of self. She is indeed a new and different person. How did she do it? She worked hard, she spent a long time in therapy, she confronted difficult problems, and she made tough decisions about unhealthy relationships. But by far the most significant ingredient in her growth was a profound encounter with God's transforming love.

Pat's story illustrates that when the love of God is consistently received by the soul, a person's life can't help but change. The love of God, modeled through the life and message of a carpenter from Nazareth, produces new and different people who are holy and good.

Yes, you must be a new and different person, holy
and good. Clothe yourself with this new nature.

EPHESIANS 4:24

38

Be Kind to Each Other

I WORK IN a building that has nine hundred people in its various offices. I don't know very many of them by name—probably fewer than fifty—but a recent experience caused me to talk with many of them.

Heading home one Friday night, I boarded one of the five elevators in our building—and promptly got stuck for an hour and fifteen minutes, all by myself. It was an awful experience, and in the following days, I found myself telling many of my "building mates" about my harrowing, claustrophobic moments. I was surprised at how kind, interested, and sympathetic they were.

"Oh, that's too bad," they would say. Or, "What did you do that whole time? You must have been worried you'd be stuck there all weekend!"

Then I got to thinking that one reason they were so kind was because they face the same emotional and physical dangers every time they get on an elevator. In light of that insight, I asked myself whether their compassion and concern were less noble and were commendable. *Do these people really care what happened to me—or are they just worried that they might get stuck sometime?* I thought.

I concluded that their gentle attitude toward me, because it was the result of their recognition of a common dilemma, represented a perfect illustration of what the apostle Paul tries to teach.

In essence, Paul says, "Remember, you're all essentially alike. The experience that one of you has today may well be the experience that others of you will have tomorrow. And just as you would like others to care deeply about your plight, care deeply about theirs."

As I ride the elevators of our building with my "friends" day to day, I keep in mind the importance of recognizing our commonalities. It always draws me close to the people with whom I talk. We discuss the weather. Sometimes we talk about how difficult Mondays are. We commiserate at the end of a long day. We celebrate Fridays. As I ride up and down with these folks, I realize I have lots in common with *every* person. Because we have so much in common, I'm challenged to treat each man and woman with kindness, respect, and courtesy—just as I'd like to be treated. My gentleness toward them has a whole lot to do with their gentleness in relation to me.

Be kind to each other, tenderhearted,
forgiving one another.

EPHESIANS 4:32

39

Pray for Yourself and
for Christians Everywhere

PASSIONATE PRAYER HAS unbelievable power!

Agnes Sanford wrote many books about prayer, and she plumbed the depths of prayer like few persons in the history of the human race. But it was her close friend and assistant Edith Drury who taught me most of what I know about prayer.

My wife, Marylyn, and I went to Maine one summer and spent ten days with Edith at her cottage on a little island off the coast. She had become an important financial donor to the school where I was the dean, and that was part of the reason we went to spend time with her, but there was a whole lot more. She told us all about her experiences as a missionary, but most of all, she drilled into our heads the essentials of effective prayer.

We prayed a lot! When Edith prayed for us, she liked to have her hands on our head or shoulders. And how she did pray! She talked to God as if He were, indeed, her own dad. She laughed with Him and pleaded with Him and agonized with Him. Most of all, she thanked Him for all the things she knew He was going to do for His people. She called this "the prayer of faith," and she was masterful in both her faith and her description of what she knew God was going to do. But at the center all of this was exuberant thanksgiving. She had so much experience with God's work in her life that she had no trouble believing magnificent things were about to happen.

Paul says to "pray all the time." Furthermore, he says to "ask God for anything in line with the Holy Spirit's wishes."

If you want to deal effectively with the little things in your life—or the monstrous things—pray all the time. Share your concerns with God. Plead with Him. Remind Him of your needs. And while you're at it, keep praying earnestly for *all* Christians everywhere.

Pray all the time. Ask God for anything in
line with the Holy Spirit's wishes. Plead with him,
reminding him of your needs, and keep praying
earnestly for all Christians everywhere.

EPHESIANS 6:18

40

Overflow with Love
for Others

THE APOSTLE PAUL had tremendous love for the people at Philippi. He said that "all my prayers for you are full of praise to God!" (Philippians 1:3). And then he said something magnificent: "When I pray for you, my heart is full of joy, because of all your wonderful help in making known the Good News about Christ from the time you first heard it until now."

After Paul finishes telling these Philippians that they "have a very special place" in his heart, he proceeds to what for him is the natural response to being saved by faith in Christ. He says, "My prayer for you is that you will overflow more and more with love for others."

Maybe you're wondering how you can "overflow" with love for others. Let me give you five suggestions:

1. List all your friends and family on a piece of paper and leave space under each name. If your list is like

mine, it will have as many as twenty-five people on it. Write a brief note about how each of these persons is doing and telephone them regularly to find out how things are going. Keep track of every one of their lives—their needs, their dreams, their special interests. For instance, my friends Les and Leslie Parrott had a baby boy a few weeks ago who was born at twenty-four weeks—sixteen weeks prior to full-term. I, along with a lot of other people, have pulled for little John Leslie Parrott, who weighed only a pound and a half at birth. And he's doing great at this point! I thank God for him and his parents.

2. Select five to eight persons to pray for passionately every day. I know a man in Orlando, Florida named Dwight Bain who prays for several Christian leaders every day, and each week on Friday he and his secretary, Gloria Leofanti, send out a page full of quotes especially designed to encourage these leaders. His example is, indeed, a good one.

3. Tell your friends about *your* special needs. Keep them up to date. For instance, I try to get all my friends praying for every one of the seminars I conduct around the country. My friend Dee Otte tells me that she and her husband, Jim, pray for every seminar. This is an enormous encouragement to me. I also tell my friends about how my partner, Greg Forgatch, and I are doing in our efforts to establish a national

matching program for single people. I tell them about everything that's going on in my life about which I need them to pray.

4. Call or write to your friends every time you come across something in the paper or a magazine, or on the radio or television, that relates to your friends' needs. Supply them with helpful or encouraging information. Go out of your way to be supportive. When you do this, you will be showing your love.

5. Offer your friends tangible help—money, groceries, or goods—if they have financial needs. The size of your gift doesn't matter; what matters is that you help in a practical way. If you give money, consider sending it in an unmarked envelope to maintain anonymity. Whatever the case, just make sure that it provides help for a specific need.

The apostle Paul knew that a great life starts with getting your roots way down deep into the soil of God's love, and it moves immediately to loving other people. When you reach out to those you care about, do it in a big, wonderful way!

My prayer for you is that you will overflow more and more with love for others.

PHILIPPIANS 1:9

41

Stop Lying to Each Other

WHEN TRUST IS broken in a relationship because of lies, the relationship is severely wounded. Every day, I deal with marriages in which two persons are aching because of the untruthfulness between them.

If I were addressing all the persons of America, especially those involved in intimate relationships, I would begin by saying: "Tell the truth! Relational health starts there. Any relationship has so much to gain if both partners can rest assured that the truth, the whole truth, and nothing but the truth is the intended goal of every message they give each other."

There are three levels on which truth-telling is crucial. The first is the *verbal* level. The trust of two people for each other can be vitally damaged if truth is not spoken. No lies should be told! Lies are verbal violations, and they erode trust significantly. If she says she didn't buy any clothes when she really did, damage is done to the relationship. If he says he didn't stop on the way home for a drink when he really did, there will be repercussions. Obviously, the more serious the infraction, the more severe the consequence on the relationship. On the other hand, if two people know in their hearts that the other person always tells the truth, the relationship has tremendous strength to draw on.

Truth is critical on the *behavioral* level. Both partners need to become people who do what they promise they'll do. If the wife says, "I'll pay the phone bill today," she should pay it today! If the husband says, "I'll meet you at First and Main at 12:00 sharp," he needs to be there on time! Trust often gets damaged in a lot of little ways, and if one or both persons consistently fail to do what they say, the relationship is compromised.

Finally, it's important to be truthful on the *being* level. This level may never get talked about, and there may never be any behavioral expressions of it, but it will be vital to the health of any developing marriage. For instance, if a marital partner pursues inner health, that person will be making a crucial "being" contribution to the relationship. But when that person gets bullied into being something he or she is not, the marriage is sure to suffer.

If you are married and you want to have an extraordinary marriage, maximize the trust factor in your relationship. If you are in a friendship, do the same.

You wonder how to do this? Tell the truth every chance you get. *Speak* the truth, *behave* the truth, and *be* the truth. If you do this, you will become known as a person of integrity. When your friend or lover relates to you, he or she will know exactly who you are. There will be no need for guessing games. Both of you can be genuine and authentic, completely free to be yourselves at the most profound levels.

> *Stop lying to each other; tell the truth,*
> *for we are parts of each other and when we lie*
> *to each other we are hurting ourselves.*
>
> EPHESIANS 4:25

42

Forge Great Partnerships

WHEN A MOM and a dad really love each other, when they treat each other with respect and honor, their whole family tends to be a "loving bunch." And when the leaders of a church really love each other, when they treat each other with esteem and sensitivity, the whole church tends to be a "loving bunch."

During my years as a psychologist, I have observed a lot of families up close, and I have also observed the inner workings of numerous churches. Church staffs often call for my assistance in dealing with challenges they currently confront. Sometimes these cases are unusually positive ones, and sometimes they have to do with major internal difficulties that the staff is facing. For instance, I want to contrast two entire church staffs with which I have worked for two entirely different reasons.

In one case, there were ten persons on the staff—from the senior pastor to the head of maintenance services—

and this staff wanted to double the impact on their community. They had a rich history and they were ready to make a major move forward. The other staff included seven ministers and staff members who weren't getting along at all well. They wanted help in achieving a sense of partnership. They faced an almost certain "break up" if they weren't able to achieve significantly greater cohesiveness.

Both groups came to me because they wanted help with their challenges, but that's where the similarities ended. The staff of ten all loved each other, and they were agreeable toward each other. The other group, however, was riddled with conflict and strife. Ultimately, the larger staff went on to be highly effective in their ministry and extremely close as coworkers. The other group, unfortunately, in time fell apart completely. The senior pastor was asked to resign his post, and the entire staff scattered "to the four winds."

Why did one group succeed and the other fail? What made the difference? I think it was four qualities:

1. The "loving" staff had a senior pastor who got along unusually well with his second in command, the "executive pastor." They had a covenant relationship with each other in which they talked through everything, supported each other in good times and bad, and responded much like nurturing, respectful parents to the rest of the staff and church.

The "staff of seven" had a senior pastor who was very much alone. He recruited the rest of the staff to equally subordinate positions, but there was no one with whom he had a close, trusting, mutually supportive relationship.

2. The staff that loved each other was more similar in personality, goals, and approach to ministry than was the contentious staff. Perhaps the successful staff started their work together with more things in common, or maybe they had been together over such a long period of time that they started thinking and acting alike. Whatever the case, they were far more similar than was the group that didn't get along.

3. The ten-member staff had developed better habits of communication and conflict resolution than had the other staff. The staff that eventually broke apart avoided difficult issues, and they never forged the kind of trust that would have allowed them to work through problems.

4. The successful staff was deeply committed to each other. Everyone had a strong sense of job security, and this enabled all of them to feel more relaxed and comfortable with the long-term prospects of their involvement together.

Interestingly, these are the very qualities that make for

great marriages and families. Successful couples have many similarities, well-developed communication, good conflict resolution skills, and solid trust.

When we love each other as Christian people and when we agree wholeheartedly with each other, we maximize our strength and our effectiveness. We become joyful in our unity. To make this happen, we need to pay close attention to the critical qualities found in great partnerships.

Then make me truly happy by loving
each other and agreeing wholeheartedly with
each other, working together with one
heart and mind and purpose.

PHILIPPIANS 2:2

43

Take a Big Interest in
Other People

I CHALLENGE YOU to try this experiment for one day:
Take a minimum of sixty seconds to ask every person you
encounter, "How are things going in your life?"

Without being obvious about it, keep the conversation
focused on the other person. Resist the urge to start talking about yourself. Develop a genuine interest in the life of
your friend or acquaintance. You will discover what millions have discovered who have tried this experiment
before you—the people in whom you take a big interest
will fall all over themselves in appreciation of you.

When I was in high school, I read Dale Carnegie's classic
book *How to Win Friends and Influence People.* I will
never forget what he said: "You can make more friends in
two months by becoming interested in other people than
you can in two years by trying to get other people interested
in you."

When you start taking an interest in other people, when

you totally focus on them, you begin to really care about what is happening in their lives. You get distracted from all the little concerns in your own life.

Do you want to make more friends? Do you want to deepen your relationships? Turn the spotlight away from your own life and onto the events, interests, and concerns of other people. You'll be amazed at how quickly these people will regard you as a true friend.

Don't just think about your own affairs,
but be interested in others, too,
and in what they are doing.

PHILIPPIANS 2:4

44

Eagerly Tell Others
the Good News

WHEN I WAS growing up, people used to tell me how important it was to "witness" to other people about my faith. It scared me. I didn't really understand what my faith was, and I didn't have the first idea of how to witness about it.

Let me tell you three things that have happened to me more recently that make me eager to tell other people about my faith:

1. I have become convinced that my *faith* is the foundation for all of my *psychology*. I find this exciting! If the genuine source of unconditional love is what God feels for every one of His "created ones," what a life-changing fact this is. I want to tell everybody about God's phenomenally positive feelings toward them.

2. I have become clear about the nature of God. I used to have such a confused sense of who God is—but

then I read in Colossians 1 that "Christ is the exact likeness of the unseen God." And in chapter 2, Paul says, "In Christ there is all of God in a human body." I suddenly became clear about God's identity. God is Jesus. To know God, all I had to do was to study the life of Christ as it is fully described in the Gospels.

3. When I got to know the man Jesus, I was overwhelmed with what I found. In the middle of a very angry, law-dominated society, He stood boldly for values that I appreciate as fundamental to healing and growth. Every story about Jesus is powerful: the woman who was brought to Him after she had been caught in the act of adultery; the parable of the prodigal son which He told to illustrate who God is; the encounter of the women who brought their children to Him and He took time out to pray for them; the man who had the withered hand that Jesus healed in spite of the anger He created in the hearts of His enemies; and the woman who touched the hem of His robe and was healed of her illness by Jesus' power and gentleness. When I discovered that God is Jesus, and Jesus is like this, I could hardly wait to tell people the good news.

Of course, some people don't want to hear all this good news, but that doesn't change the news, and their response isn't final. Sometimes it takes certain life conditions to create the right environment for that news to sprout within their hearts.

✦

Now I enjoy telling people about the gospel. As a psychologist, I know that God's love for people is exactly what they need in order to become the persons God created them to be. When they are authentic persons—and only then—they have a chance to experience the kind of internally magnificent life Jesus called "abundant."

Make the most of your chances to
tell others the Good News. Be wise in
all your contacts with them.

COLOSSIANS 4:5

45

Hunger for the Truth

I HAVE KNOWN Debby for several years. She has been in my Monday-night therapy group longer than any other person has. The truth is, she doesn't need to come anymore. For months I have told her she is one of the healthiest people I know, but she keeps coming because this group has become her family. Besides, she continues to grow.

Through the years of Debby's therapy I have watched one of her qualities develop tremendously—she may have more respect for the truth than any other person I know. Whereas some people might shade the truth to get out of an awkward situation or to cast themselves in a better light, Debby demonstrates integrity and precision in everything she says. Whereas some people might betray a hint of pretension or phoniness, Debby is unfailingly forthright and candid. There is not a whiff of falsehood about her.

When you ask Debby a tough question—one that has the potential of making her look "bad"—she takes plenty of time to formulate her answer. She may ask a few questions of her own, and then she may collect more information from inside herself—from her thoughts and feelings. Then she delivers her answer. Time after time, she amazes me! Her answers are not only insightful, but they seem so exact and unequivocal as well.

I guarantee that when you encounter those rare individuals who are dedicated to the whole truth in any given moment, you will note that they are in touch with their deepest and most profound inner parts. They are being fully themselves, and this is what authenticity is all about.

I marvel at the fact that the truth is always friendlier than anything less than the truth. When the truth is "on the table," the anxiety always goes down rather than up. I often have a difficult time convincing myself and my clients of this fact, but I consider it of the greatest importance.

For instance, in a marriage, both partners have so much to gain if they can rest assured that the truth, the whole truth, and nothing but the truth is the intended goal of every message they give each other.

Tell the truth! It all starts here. It leads inevitably to trust. And trust is the "emotional stuff" in which every human relationship thrives.

*We will lovingly follow the truth at all times—
speaking truly, dealing truly, living truly—and so*

❧

become more and more in every way like Christ
who is the Head of his body, the Church.

EPHESIANS 4:15

46

Develop a Vital Union
with Christ

ONE OF THE most revealing stories in all the New Testament focuses on Jesus' close friends Mary and Martha.

Martha worked so hard! She was convinced that her reason for being involved accomplishment. She entertained guests, cooked for them, cleaned up after them, and there was nothing she wasn't willing to do.

Unfortunately for Martha, her sister, Mary, had a different idea about what's most important in life. She stayed close to Jesus. When He was around, she was right by Him.

Eventually, Martha had had enough. She came to Jesus and said, "Sir, doesn't it seem unfair to you that my sister just sits here while I do all the work? Tell her to come and help me" (Luke 10:40).

The way Jesus replied to Martha is crucial for us. He said, "Martha, dear friend, you are so upset over all these details! There is really only one thing worth being concerned about. Mary has discovered it—and I won't take it away from her!" (Luke 10:41–42).

The key to living a fulfilling, satisfying life is getting into a right relationship with God. And the key to getting into a right relationship with God is to spend a lot of time around Jesus. Paul stresses that the way to do this is to "live in vital union with Christ."

A client of mine named Lisa spends considerable time cultivating her faith. Before she started doing this, her marriage was a complete mess. She used to argue with her husband, belittle him at every opportunity, and try to make him feel as bad as he made her feel. As you can imagine, their marriage was sick. Then she had a whole new spiritual renewal.

"My cousin talked me into going to a conference at her church," she told me. "I can only tell you that God spoke to me through the speaker. I saw how rotten I had been acting toward my husband. Most of all, I realized that I had been ignoring God."

As a result, she began spending more and more time "living in vital union with Christ."

"I can't believe the difference this has made in my attitude, my outlook on life, and especially my marriage," Lisa said. "We've still got a lot of problems to work through, but now I *want* to work through them. My heart has softened toward my husband, and I feel so much more love for him now."

When you develop a deep, abiding relationship with

❧

Christ, everything about your relationship with others changes. Why? Because everything about your relationship with *yourself* becomes more positive and healthy. The clear secret: Live in *vital* union with Christ!

> *And now just as you trusted Christ to save you,*
> *trust him, too, for each day's problems;*
> *live in vital union with him.*

COLOSSIANS 2:6

47

Influence People Through Your Humility

DR. EARL V. PULLIAS was the highly esteemed, long-time dean of Pepperdine University. Then he became professor of higher education at the University of Southern California. He had a powerful influence on hundreds of lives. Let me tell you why he was so influential.

He was a penetrating thinker and a captivating speaker. What he had to say was so substantive and insightful that people paid close attention whenever he spoke. He received one standing ovation after another for his lectures, scores of letters about the influence he'd had on young lives, and nearly every honor that his world could offer him. An educational psychologist by training, he wrote several acclaimed books. Though these accolades didn't seem important to him, he accepted them with the grace and modesty that characterized everything he did. Still, his speaking, writing, and expertise were just a small part of his fame.

He was most famous for how he chose to live his life. A gentle, tenderhearted man, he accumulated almost no worldly possessions. He rode a bicycle back and forth to work for many years, not because he needed the exercise, but because he had never purchased a car.

What's more, Dr. Pullias and his wife, Pauline, could have purchased a big house in some upscale area, but they continued to live in the little home they had purchased in the 1930s. Over time, that part of Los Angeles had become poor and run-down, but he stayed anyway. Why? Because he believed in staying where he could make a difference—among the people and in the neighborhood where he had lived for so many years. In fact, he lived in that same place up until his death a few years ago.

Earl Pullias was a brilliant man who, as the apostle Paul says, chose to "lay aside his mighty power" and to "take the disguise of a slave."

Humility, when it is genuine, is wonderfully attractive. When an individual is so internally secure that he can live simply and modestly, focusing his energy and attention on "weightier matters," everyone he encounters is sure to recognize the Spirit of God at work.

It was certainly like this for Dean Earl V. Pullias.

Your attitude should be the kind
that was shown us by Jesus Christ, who,
though he was God, did not demand and cling to
his rights as God, but laid aside his mighty power

*and glory, taking the disguise of a slave and
becoming like men . . . Yet it was because of
this that God raised him up to the heights
of heaven and gave him a name which
is above every other name.*

PHILIPPIANS 2:5–7, 9

48

❦

Tap into the Treasures of Wisdom and Knowledge

NEUROLOGICAL PSYCHOLOGISTS have estimated that the human brain has as many as two billion megabytes of capacity. If we can ever learn to maximize the potential of this giant computer, all kinds of wonderful things will happen.

For instance, one of my favorite writers was Norman Cousins, whose most famous book, *Anatomy of an Illness,* chronicled his battle with cancer. At midlife, he contracted the disease and was expected to die. Rather than undergo the normal course of treatment, he devised his own regimen. He began listening to comedy tapes and viewing hilarious old movies that made him laugh uproariously. And it wasn't long until doctors had determined that his cancer was in remission.

Dr. Cousins became the head of a major program at UCLA to study this phenomenon. After several years of careful investigation, he came to the conclusion that the human brain is the largest pharmaceutical storehouse in the world. It has more chemicals and combinations of chemicals than any single pharmaceutical source currently available. Dr. Cousins believed that any ailment confronting human beings can be healed if they can learn how to release the necessary chemicals into the bloodstream.

The fact is that when we learn how to help human beings discover the potential God created them to have, the kingdom of God will be magnificently furthered.

And talk about releasing your brain to do phenomenal things! When you understand the importance of Christ in your life, you will trigger the release of chemicals—and, of course, you will release spiritual power—which will bring incredible understanding, wisdom, and knowledge.

I have no doubt that you can learn to bring your creativity to bear on any problem you encounter, learn to manage enormous challenges, and become so skilled in your personal relationships and professional pursuits that other people will want to know your "secret." All of this will depend on your actualizing the potential God has created within you. This potential, located in your extraordinary brain, gets released when you receive the powerful message of the gospel.

In him lie hidden all the mighty, untapped
treasures of wisdom and knowledge.

COLOSSIANS 2:3

49

Make This Your Ultimate Goal:
To Be Filled with Christ

I SEE TWENTY-FIVE to thirty people in psychotherapy every week. Nearly every person who comes to me has a dominant theme that directs his or her conversation with me.

For instance, I am counseling a man and a woman—I'll call them David and Terri—who are trying to get their marriage back on track. They have lived separately for several years, and just when it looked like their marriage was going to end for good, Terri invited David to seek therapy as "one last try."

Every week when I see them, David has to get beyond the business problems that regularly confront him. He can't focus on his marriage until he clears the everyday clutter out of the way. Once he does, he pursues the central questions for him: Can he trust this woman again? Can he believe the future will be better than the past with her?

And Terri pursues some of her recurring issues, too.

Will David treat her more sensitively in the future than he did in the past? Will he allow her to be more authentically herself—to live her own life? Will he stop expecting her to acquiesce to his every whim and wish?

These are valid questions, but when they are replayed over and over without resolution, it only keeps David and Terri mired in the past. They can't move forward. So I keep pushing them to address issues that will prepare them to relate a thousand times more effectively with each other.

"When you learn to be happy deep within you," I tell them, "and when you achieve emotional health, it will help your individual lives and your relationship immensely. You will be able to resolve conflicts in a way that's honoring to both of you. You will be able to manage anger productively. And you won't expect your partner to be the source of your contentment."

We are making progress! They are slowly becoming released from the old hurts and grudges that divided them in the past. They are starting to see that they do not hold for each other the ultimate power. They are beginning to recognize that their own internal freedom and security are the consequence of their relationship with God.

If David and Terri finally get this straight, it will take enormous stress off their marriage. They won't keep looking to each other for the emotional satisfaction they so desperately seek. They will begin getting their personal needs met in a far more satisfying way.

❦

Ideally, the time will come when they will each be filled with God Himself. Then they will be able to love each other far more effectively. They will free their marriage from the bondage that always comes when individuals think only their marriage partner can provide emotional love. Since their marriage partner could never meet their most profound needs—the needs only God can satisfy—this approach is always doomed to failure. Unfortunately, the marriage often gets abandoned in the process.

What a happy discovery it is to realize that our salvation comes with being filled full of Christ.

> *. . . until finally we all believe alike about our salvation and about our Savior, God's Son, and all become full-grown in the Lord—yes, to the point of being filled full with Christ.*
>
> EPHESIANS 4:13

50

Believe That God Knows What Is Best for Us at All Times

ONE OF THE finest secretaries I ever had, Lynda Sittser, was killed in a violent automobile accident a few years ago. The car in which she and her family were riding was hit head-on by a vehicle driven by a drunk driver. The collision killed not only Lynda, but one of her children and her mother-in-law as well.

Lynda's husband, Professor Gerald L. Sittser of Whitworth College in Spokane, Washington, has written a magnificent book about this tragedy entitled *A Grace Disguised: How the Soul Grows Through Loss*. A man of compelling faith, he was behind the wheel that day when the violent collision occurred. Through the years, he and his surviving three children have had to work through their overwhelming grief caused by this event.

How could Dr. Sittser and his children ever come to believe that God "understands us and knows what is best for us at all times"? Could they really affirm the apostle

Paul's words when he says, "And we know that all that happens to us is working for our good if we love God and are fitting into his plans" (Romans 8: 28)?

In his book, Dr. Sittser poignantly describes the process through which he had to pass. Finally, he is able to say, along with his loved ones:

> If your soul aches, you may be on a journey that will stretch your faith, your understanding of the meaning of life, and your knowledge of God. If you let it, your sorrow will increase your capacity to live well, to love life, and to experience joy, not *after* the darkness but even in the midst of it.

The power of the Christian faith is that it isn't bound by the limitations of time as we understand it. It extends our understanding into eternity, and this makes everything so much easier to manage about our lives and our fortunes. That is why Paul can go on to say in Romans 8:38, "For I am convinced that nothing can ever separate us from his love. Death can't, and life can't."

When we believe with certainty that we can never be separated from God's love, everything about our daily lives takes on a different perspective. When we *really* believe this, even during the chaotic moments of our days, it changes our outlook on the major crises that wound us deeply as well as the little problems that rattle us along the way.

❦

*He has showered down upon us the richness
of his grace—for how well he understands us and
knows what is best for us at all times.*

EPHESIANS 1:8

51

❧

Pursue Peace

THE IDEA OF "peace" is a powerful one for the apostle
Paul. This peace always has to do with personal relationships—a person's relationship to himself, to his fellow
human beings, and to God. For Paul, peace is always
"born of reconciliation"—that is, being reconciled to
God. Once this happens through Christ, it can then happen *within* any individual and *between* people.

The ultimate meaning of "peace" is "a state of tranquillity or quiet." It denotes a "freedom from disquieting
or oppressive thoughts or emotions." Isn't that exactly
what we all want in life? When little things hound us—the
refrigerator conks out, bills pile up, the car needs to be
replaced, deadlines nag at us—don't we long for tranquillity and quiet? When problems, hassles, and nuisances
surround us day after day and week after week, don't we
wish for deep-down calm and serenity?

Paul says we can have this kind of peace—in Christ.
Review Paul's thinking with me:

- Christ *is* God.

- This God knows us intimately—better than we know ourselves.

- He loves us to the marrow of our bones.

- He is ready to forgive us for the mess we've made of trying to be our own god.

- He invites us into a relationship that will last throughout eternity.

- He promises us a home with Him in heaven.

- He encourages us not to place too much importance on the things of this life.

- He pleads with us to enjoy our living and to experience peace at the center of it.

When I work with people in psychotherapy, my goal is to help them fully acknowledge and understand this kind of thinking. I know that when people find peace, all the annoying, upsetting "stuff" of their lives becomes very small. They can simply rest easy and enjoy all the positive things in their lives.

For Christ himself is our way of peace.

EPHESIANS 2:14

52

❧

Choose the Right Model

WHEN I WAS a young boy, my dad led the singing for our church. I well remember how he would stand at the front, hold the songbook in his left hand, and lead the congregation by keeping time with his right hand.

One of my earliest memories is of standing by my dad when I was about three years old. Family members told me that I would often grab hold of Dad's leg with my left arm and mimic him with my waving right arm—making sure to lead that congregation with all I had.

What a powerful impact experiences like that one must have on us.

I just returned from doing another seminar this weekend in Tulsa, Oklahoma. During the course of the seminar, I told one of my favorite stories about my dad.

When I was very young, my dad made sure that my two sisters and I attended every service of the church (my mother was nearly as dedicated to this principle, but it was my dad whose leadership was most obvious).

What I like about my memory of church attendance, though, has little to do with the sense of obligation that he placed in my heart. It has much more to do with the attractiveness of his caring and "entertaining" spirit in the middle of those long and complex sermons I sat through as a very young boy.

He would reach into his pocket and pull out something to share with me—something like Sen-Sens—little candies that provided a break from all of the seriousness. Sometimes, he would write me a note. Now and then, when the sermon was *way* over my head, he would make out some addition problems that I could work to keep myself stimulated (as a matter of fact, I learned most of what I know about mathematics from my dad during church services when my mind was too young to understand).

He did the same kind of thing for our daughters when they were young. Maybe that's why he is, without any question, the relative they mention most often to their own children—the person they want their kids to understand as they do.

As I write this essay I am reminded of Paul's encouragement that we treat God as a much loved child treats his father. Paul says to make God our model.

After thinking about my own dad, I immediately think of that father in Jesus' story who runs down the road when he sees his son coming home.

We will *never* go wrong if we study everything in

Scripture about the kind of person God is and make Him our example.

Follow God's example in everything you do just as
a much loved child imitates his father.

EPHESIANS 5:1

53

"Just Say No" to the World's Ideas About How to Be Saved

IN THE ENVIRONMENT you grew up in, what did you need in order to feel good about yourself? What did you have to do and be to feel accepted by others and yourself?

Did you have to be in the popular crowd? Did you have to make the cheerleading squad? Did you need to be first-string on the football team? Did you need to drive a car that everyone thought was impressive?

Did you need to go with one of the prettiest girls or one of the most handsome boys? Did you need to come from a big home on the right side of the tracks? Did you need to be smart, get good grades, and be "college material"? Did you need to wear great clothes and have plenty of money?

Well, whatever it was we needed to feel good about ourselves—and however well we did at it—most of us sense that we fell short of the prize. It's hard to meet the idealized social standard for feeling good about yourself. Don't you agree?

The fact is, though, that all of these strategies are worthless. They wouldn't work when you were growing up, and they won't work now. The Christian faith is about your freedom to say no to all the external criteria for establishing your worth and value.

If you want to go to school for years to earn degrees and increase your knowledge, that's fine. If you want to wear fashionable clothes, drive a fancy car, and live in a nice house, that's fine! But you don't need any of those things to feel good about yourself.

The Christian faith says simply this: You be you in all your genuineness—and that's enough.

Recognize that the person you really are is the person you'll have the most fun being. The person you really are is the person who, when you are true to him or her, you will get the most enjoyment out of being.

Thank God for freedom from all the old frustrating expectations and standards. You don't have to be better-looking than everybody else. You don't have to be one of the top athletes. You don't have to be a campus beauty queen. You don't have to be rich. You don't have to be brilliant.

You don't have to be anything in order to feel good about yourself. All you must do is accept the fact that you need only be the person you *really* are. That's what Christ sets you free to be.

*Since you died, as it were, with Christ and this has
set you free from following the world's ideas of how
to be saved—by doing good and obeying various
rules—why do you keep right on following them
anyway, still bound by such rules?*

COLOSSIANS 2:20

54

Learn What Pleases
the Lord

IT SEEMS AS if it has taken most of my life to get clear about what the Lord wants from me. If I had it to do all over again, I would want to do five things earlier:

1. I would want to read *The Living Bible* much earlier in my life. (Of course, this means that Mr. Ken Taylor, founder of Tyndale House Publishing Company, would have had to finish writing *The Living Bible* much earlier in *his* life.) This incredible paraphrase of the Bible has changed my life enormously. If you don't have a Bible that makes sense to you, get a *Living Bible*. No other version of the Bible has had as much influence on me or the persons I know best. More copies of this version have sold than any translation or paraphrase of the Bible except for the *King James Version*.

2. I would read the New Testament through one hundred times by the time I was twenty. Perhaps I wouldn't have been mature enough to understand all the deep meanings—but what a difference it would have meant to my life! I would have understood so much earlier how much I am loved by the very God who created me, and I would have known how passionately He wishes for me to love all of the persons He has created.

3. I would have led seminars on important life topics much earlier in my career. It is through conducting seminars that I have a chance to talk with people about every issue under the sun. This causes me to study Scripture, to read dozens of other sources, and to develop answers to crucial questions. I am reminded that the apostle Paul in his travels always went from synagogue to synagogue, where he faced all kinds of questions. Responding to these questions, he developed his own faith. Then he was able to write magnificent letters. I especially think of his letter to the church at Rome, which stands as such a pillar of Christian teaching.

4. I would spend more time with little children and older people at an earlier age. Marylyn and I now have nine grandchildren, and they have taught us many profound things about our faith. When they sit

around our family dinner table, several of them want to offer the prayer of thanks for the food. And in these prayers I learn important truths just as I used to when my ninety-year-old dad would pray before our larger family's meal.

5. I would sing the old gospel songs over and over from an earlier age. There is something about those songs, many of them with exact words from Scripture, that brings so much enlightenment about who God is and what He wants from us. When you sing "Blessed assurance, Jesus is mine, Oh what a foretaste of Glory Divine," or "Beneath the cross of Jesus, I feign would take my stand," what an uplift it gives to your life.

The key to the great Christian life is learning what makes God happy. His happiness is our best indicator of how well we are living our lives.

Learn as you go along what pleases the Lord.

EPHESIANS 5:10

55

Spend Your Time on Things
That Matter

IMAGINE THAT THERE are five things you can do today:

1. You can sit at home and watch your favorite baseball team play against their number one rival, and the game will determine which team goes to the World Series.

2. You can work at your job, and you will be paid triple-time. You stand to make an enormous amount of money in one day.

3. You can take a long walk in a beautiful park with the love of your life and talk about things that evoke romantic thoughts within you.

4. You can read a great book and be whisked off to a life in distant times in a faraway land, and the story will fill you with excitement and adventure.

5. You can travel to a nearby town and walk with a crowd of people who are listening to a man tell stories. The man's name is Jesus. He is a carpenter from a local community, and He has an incredible way of zeroing in on the great questions of life.

I don't know about you, but my excitement is centered on trying to get to know the carpenter from Nazareth. I want to get to know Him as well as I can, spend as much time with Him as possible, listen to every word He says, watch Him under every condition, and try my best to make my own life like His.

What about you? Can you imagine finding one of these alternatives more appealing than number five? Or are you with me—does number five sound exactly like what you would want to do?

Maybe you're already aware that when Jesus left the earth, He gave us a way of knowing Him that does not require going to a neighboring community. If we read the Scriptures, pray for the action of the Holy Spirit in our lives, and open our minds and hearts to Him, He will become as real to us as He would have if He were on earth this very day.

The apostle Paul says that there is simply nothing like it. He calls the experience of knowing Jesus Christ, his Lord, *priceless!* In fact, he says that everything else is worthless compared to this.

If you agree with Paul, as I do, then we need to get about the process of making Him our closest friend.

Yes, everything else is worthless
when compared with the priceless gain
of knowing Christ Jesus my Lord. I have put aside
all else, counting it worth less than nothing,
in order that I can have Christ.

PHILIPPIANS 3:8

56

Let Christ's Mighty Power
Work Within You

WHEN ARE YOU most powerful? I'm talking about any kind of power—physical, emotional, interpersonal, marital, moral, or economic.

The greatest example of power in all of Scripture has to do with the mighty power that brought Christ back to life again after He died. I never cease to be amazed at the idea that "this same power can operate within our lives." And when it does, we are empowered to do all the things we are capable of doing.

In his book *The Transforming Moment,* Professor James Loder of Princeton Theological Seminary tells the story of how he and his wife stopped along the highway to help two ladies whose car was stranded with a flat tire. Dr. Loder pulled his camper to a stop fifteen feet in front of the other vehicle, got out of his car, and knelt by the car's right front fender.

Suddenly, an ear-splitting screech of brakes came from

behind him. A sixty-four-year-old man who had "never had an accident in his life." fell asleep at the wheel. Breaking only for an instant, he rammed the car from behind and shoved it over on top of Dr. Loder. He tells what happened next:

> Because the two women who had been traveling together had also been injured in the accident, there was no one to help but my wife. Arlene is a slight woman, barely over five feet tall. With her hands under the bumper, she prayed, "In the name of Jesus Christ, in the name of Jesus Christ . . ." Recounting this event later, she said that when her strength in the heaving effort began to give way, she partially lost consciousness for a few seconds; when she was able to refocus her attention, she was surprised to see that the car had been lifted.

Professor Loder sustained serious injuries in the accident: "I later learned that my right thumb had been torn off at the first joint, five ribs were broken, the left lung was bleeding, and my skin was gouged and scraped from head to foot."

But miraculously, his life was spared, and his entire ministry became different. When he was caught in a life-threatening moment, his wife had cried out to God. She was filled with His mighty power, and her strength was multiplied beyond imagination.

When God's power invades our lives, enormous energy

❧

fills our entire psychological and physical systems. We can do things we never thought possible.

Can you have this energy? Absolutely! How do you get it? When you have faith in Christ and you trust in Him alone.

Then you are filled with an explosive power that enables you to reach—and even surpass—the potential of all your gifts and abilities. It all starts with getting yourself free from old entanglements, then building a solid self-concept based on God's incredible view of you, and moving through your life trusting in Christ to empower you.

Now I have given up everything else—
I have found it to be the only way to really know
Christ and to experience the mighty power
that brought him back to life again.

PHILIPPIANS 3:10

57

Plant Your Roots in the Most Fertile Soil of All

LET'S TALK ABOUT "roots," and then we'll talk about *your* roots in particular.

I've been fascinated by roots ever since I was a small boy growing up in Iowa. My mother encouraged me to plant a vegetable garden every year, and I remember becoming engrossed in the root systems of carrots, radishes, and turnips at an early age.

I recall my teacher in that Iowa country school, Miss Gardner, telling Carol Weaver and me (the only two students in our class) that roots hold plants in place, dissolve salts from the soil, and transport water and nutrients. She explained that roots most often grow in the ground but that they can flourish in water or even in air.

Roots have a complex and strategic makeup. For instance, root hairs grow from the outermost edge of the rootlet, and they are like tiny mouths that drink in water from the spaces around the particles of soil.

But enough about roots and a demonstration of what a grade-schooler in a country school learned many years ago.

Think about *your* roots. I'm not talking about your heritage, your family roots, but your life roots, which anchor you and take in nourishment for you. What kind of soil are your roots in, and what kind of nourishment are they extracting for your benefit?

For instance, if you spend all your time at work, I assume that your roots will extract whatever it is that your work provides: Money? A sense of achievement? Social interaction? A place to belong?

And if your roots are planted in the life you encounter on your television set, the "nourishment" you obtain will probably depend on the programs you watch. If you watch comedy shows, your roots may supply you with some short-term entertainment, a chance to unwind for a minute, but mostly nonsense. If you watch educational programs, your roots may help to expand your world.

The apostle Paul encourages us to sink our roots into Christ and draw nourishment from Him. What are you likely to get by extending your roots into Christ?

He will secure your place in the world. He says that you are created by Him, that you are totally unique, that if you trust Him, you will live forever. He secures your place here on earth and in heaven.

The more you run your roots down into Him, the more you recognize your own lovability. Christ makes it clear that He just flat out loves you and enjoys you, and He wants you to love and enjoy yourself. He doesn't want you to feel anxious and worried. He certainly doesn't want you to wallow in guilt or suffer from depression. Put your roots down into this Christ and discover how much love suddenly becomes available to you.

Also, when you become rooted in Christ, you feel empowered to do tremendous things. All of a sudden, you have all the resources to accomplish whatever it is that strikes you as important to do. Your roots supply you with energy, a mighty power, and more physiological and emotional capacity than you can even imagine.

What a way for us to get ourselves secured, loved, and empowered!

Let your roots grow down into him and
draw up nourishment from him.

COLOSSIANS 2:7

58

Be Controlled by the
Holy Spirit

How can you tell for sure if you're allowing the Spirit of God to control your life? Simply examine your attitudes, your emotions, your actions, and your interactions with others.

A few years ago, I memorized Galatians 5:22–23. I have repeated these verses in my mind countless times. The nine qualities listed in these verses—what are commonly called the "fruits of the Spirit"—have become imprinted on my brain. I ask myself frequently how I'm doing in opening my soul to the Spirit of God. And when I ask this question, I move immediately to an inventory of these qualities in my life.

For instance, when I get perturbed at another driver and act rudely toward him or her, I know that I have squeezed the Spirit out of my life. When I get gloomy and let a dark mood pervade my thoughts, squashing all the joy in my life, I realize I've done it again.

Sometimes the Christian life seems complex, but it isn't really. The apostle Paul gives us a clear barometer to know if God is moving in our lives. We simply evaluate how patient we are with our spouse at the end of a long, stressful day. We assess how gently we respond when our kids are noisy and boisterous because they're enjoying each other. We check and see how faithful we are in relation to friends who are going through a difficult, painful experience. We look at how kind we are to the janitor who cleans our office after hours. We ask ourselves how much peace we have in our lives.

When you put on your pajamas at night, flop into your bed, and arrange your pillow under your head, you can take the proven, reliable inventory all over again. And if you discover you aren't doing so well in relation to the nine "fruitful ingredients," breathe that conscious prayer to God to come in and fill you with His presence. His own faithfulness is such that He is always ready to be your constant companion.

But when the Holy Spirit controls
our lives he will produce this kind of fruit in us:
love, joy, peace, patience, kindness, goodness,
faithfulness, gentleness and self-control.

GALATIANS 5:22–23

59

Understand What Matters in
Life and What Doesn't

WHEN PROMISE KEEPERS met in Washington, D.C., during that exciting weekend in October of 1997, one million men representing every height, weight, color, socioeconomic background, denomination, marital status, educational level, and verbal ability were in that crowd.

I noted that there were some men present who were huge, with big muscles and broad shoulders. And I noted that there were plenty of small, skinny people there as well. Some persons were fit and athletic-looking, and others were crippled—and had been for life. As I looked around and saw such a diversity of people, I thought how heaven will be full of every kind of person—every shape, every color, every nationality.

What great fortune that Christ is equally available to us all! Even with all our differences, we have so many of the same desperate needs. What Christ brings to one man or woman, He brings to *every* man and woman. And it is *every* man and woman on the face of the earth who needs exactly what Christ has to give.

As Colossians 3:11 says, "Whether a person has Christ is what matters." That's because He is the only one who can provide everything required to save your soul.

So it really doesn't matter whether you are black or white, brown or yellow, whether you are highly educated or not educated at all, whether you have an outgoing personality or are painfully shy. Paul says that nationality, race, education, and social position are meaningless.

Christ is equally available to persons of all races, economic brackets, personality types, and social status. If you find yourself on an angry sea with nothing to hang on to, Christ stands ready to help. He won't ask any questions. He won't check your credentials. He will only offer His help. Whoever you are, wherever you come from, He is there to personally assist you.

In this new life one's nationality or race
or education or social position is unimportant;
such things mean nothing. Whether a person
has Christ is what matters, and he
is equally available to all.

COLOSSIANS 3:11

60

Recognize That Your Real Life Is in Heaven

I DON'T KNOW what heaven looks like, and I assume you don't either. But God tells us that everything about it will make us glad we're there.

In Colossians 3:1, Paul says you should "set your sights on the rich treasures and joys of heaven where [Christ] sits beside God in the place of honor and power."

My wife, Marylyn, and I visited the Hawaiian island of Lanai last year, and we had the time of our lives. We looked out on water that was bluer than blue. We walked along the sandy white beaches as gentle breezes cooled us off. We breathed in the salt air and dipped our toes in the warm surf. We ate scrumptious meals as we watched waves roll in and out. We played tennis and golf to our hearts' delight.

We often call such places "paradise"—but you can bet heaven is a billion times better than the island of Lanai! Where have you been in the world that was beautiful and pristine? Heaven will be a whole lot better than that.

It recently occurred to me that if we were to poll all the fetuses in all the wombs of all the potential mothers in the world to see if they wanted to travel through the birth canal and enter the big world, the vote would probably be overwhelmingly negative. I can imagine them saying, "Leave the warm, secure haven of my mother's womb and enter that scary, dangerous world? Forget it!" And yet, having been born, an overwhelming majority of persons would celebrate their lives. Facing the same question all over again, they probably wouldn't want to miss being born.

I'm sure that dying to this life in order to be raised up to a new life in heaven is very much like that. We get so nervous and concerned about death, but when we arrive in heaven, we will undoubtedly be thrilled beyond measure that we're there.

Let heaven fill your thoughts; don't spend your time worrying about things down here.

COLOSSIANS 3:2

61

❦

Don't Worry About Making a Good Impression on Others

I HAVE HAD three people in psychotherapy through the years who illustrate three different ways of "not worrying about making a good impression on others."

1. I saw a client named John for several years, and he seemed intent on making a bad impression on others. He just plain didn't like people—and he couldn't care less if others liked him. His conversations were salted with sarcastic remarks, and he took advantage of every opportunity to start an argument. He got himself into trouble with everybody he encountered. John was so wounded from his early life that he went around making enemies everywhere he went.

2. I had a middle-aged woman in therapy who had no particular ax to grind with other people, but it didn't matter really what others thought. She had no interest in other people. They were irrelevant to her life. This woman, though, was not doing what the apostle Paul insists that

we try to do. In her indifference to other people, she demonstrated no concern for them at all. The apostle encourages us not to make other people authorities in our lives, but still to be deeply sensitive to their needs.

3. The woman who really caught the secret was seventy-three years old when I started seeing her. She genuinely loved other people, but she was absolutely intent on being obedient to God and becoming the genuine person God called her to be. She served and cared for others, and she made every effort to be patient, kind, and tenderhearted. She didn't try to make a good impression on others, but she loved them through and through.

When the apostle Paul tells us not to worry about making a good impression, he certainly isn't suggesting we should be aloof, detached, and uninterested in others. He doesn't mean we should be antisocial like my client John, or unconcerned about other people like the second person I mentioned. Paul does mean we are to strive for authenticity and genuineness in our lives in spite of what others may think. At the same time, we are to be tenderhearted and kind, ready to suffer even for those same people whose opinion of us is not all that crucial—only because we have found our wholeness and acceptance in the God who created us.

Don't worry about making a good impression on
them but be ready to suffer quietly and patiently.

COLOSSIANS 3:12

62

Become Wise About
Spiritual Things

THERE HAS BEEN a dramatic resurgence of spirituality all over North America. The November 28, 1994 issue of *Newsweek* focused on this heightened interest in spiritual things:

> From Wall Streeters to artists, from Andre Agassi to David Mamet, millions of Americans are embarking on a search for the sacred in their lives. Whether out of dissatisfaction with the material world or worried about the coming millennium, they are seeking to put spirituality back in their lives. For careerist baby boomers, it's even OK to use the "S" words—soul, sacred, spiritual, sin.

For better or worse, there are scores of spiritual paths people take to deal with the profound questions of life. In a stimulating speech given by Norman Lear, the popular television producer, at the National Press Club in December of 1993, many of the "spiritual paths" people take were identified and described. Lear believes that throughout North America, there is a "buzzing, disconnected eruption of spiritual reaction to our times." He believes that this quest for spiritual significance is the most powerful theme of our culture.

The apostle Paul says to ask God to make you *wise about spiritual things.* The fact is that spirituality can lead us in many different directions, but if it doesn't lead us to the one true God, it will be *mis*leading and ultimately tragic for our souls.

In a poll of 756 adults that appeared in the same issue of *Newsweek* cited earlier, 60 percent of those questioned said they think "a person needs to believe in God in order to experience the sacred," and 50 percent reported that they "feel a deep sense of the sacred all or most of the time in church or at worship services." Outside of church, 45 percent sense the sacred during meditation, 68 percent at the birth of a child, and 26 percent during sex.

For the apostle Paul, God is always at the center of the *wise* spiritual quest.

Having been raised on biblical, Judeo-Christian teachings, my own spiritual quest has always centered on God. But it was long after I became a psychologist that I began to understand more deeply, and believe more passionately, in God. My passion was ignited when I began to study more fully the writings of the New Testament. I discovered there a description of God—in the life and teachings of Jesus—that I find irresistibly attractive.

It may be that 58 percent of all Americans "feel the need to experience spiritual growth," but I am convinced that only when this quest is centered on the true God, who *is* love and the *source* of love, will it lead to emotional and relational wholeness. But when the quest is less organized and less focused, when it does not center on this loving God, the quest usually stagnates well before a person has arrived at the goal of emotional health.

The spiritual side of life is so compelling, so attractive, so powerful. All we need in order to be wise about this crucial area is to make sure that God is at the center of it.

Ask God to make you wise
about spiritual things.

COLOSSIANS 1:9

63

Keep Working Hard to Fulfill
Your Potential

CONSIDERING THAT THE human brain has two billion megabytes of capacity, most of us have a lot of potential that is yet to be actualized. This potential exists in dozens of different areas, and the degree of potential you have in each area is probably beyond your own imagination.

One of the exciting aspects of life is trying to develop a little more of our potential every day. Sometimes the part of us that we want to develop seems uncooperative. We may even think that we simply can't grow in one area or another. I am frequently reminded of what my favorite golfer, Arnold Palmer, once said: "The most rewarding things you do in life are often the ones that look like they cannot be done."

If you want to add richness to your life, take on three or four areas in which you wish to grow. Make them areas that really matter to you, and make sure that you care a lot about any growth you experience in these areas. Nothing will fill you with more excitement than to know on a daily basis that you are making progress in the development of the potential that has always been within you.

Now and then, you will achieve something phenomenal. You will become, for instance, the master of your anger. You will learn how to use your "physiological preparedness," what we label as *anger,* to do some magnificent things in your life. Or you may learn how to attain deep-down peace in your life. This peace will likely show itself in sleep patterns that are significantly better, or eating patterns that are healthier, or drinking patterns that are under greater control.

Obviously, you may take on something simpler, such as gardening, golf, tennis, writing, or any one of a thousand other things. These things, too, can enrich your life and give you a sense of accomplishment.

I encourage you to make a list of all the ways in which you would like to "grow yourself." And then realize that you can take enormous strides in becoming that person you would like to be.

When you are clear about the person you are capable of becoming, and when you develop a burning desire to see this magnificent person become more and more actualized, you will experience a pervasive sense of excitement for living.

I keep working toward that day when I will finally
be all that Christ saved me for and wants me to be.

PHILIPPIANS 3:12

64

✣

Unwrap the
Gifts God Gives You

IMAGINE THAT YOU awaken one morning to find three beautifully wrapped presents sitting on your bedside table. When you open the first, you immediately experience overwhelming inner peace. You feel a total sense of reconciliation with every person you know. More than that, you feel reconciled with God. You experience tranquillity and contentment that you have never known before.

I assume that you would be ecstatic, overjoyed, given to shouting, dancing, and celebrating throughout the house and the neighborhood.

And then you remember the second gift waiting to be opened. Unwrapping it, you are immediately filled with love for every single person in the world. You love yourself, you love every member of your family, you love your neighbors, and you even love your enemies. You wish the best for people everywhere, and you are filled with compassion for people who suffer hardship.

I assume that you would be beside yourself again, filled to the brim with the desire to tell everybody you know about the love you have for them.

Finally, you reach for the third present. Opening it, your faith in God reaches unbelievable heights. He is as real to you as your breathing, as close to you as your thoughts. You know beyond the shadow of any doubt that you can trust Him with every ounce of your being.

I assume that you would want to travel the highways and byways telling every person about your faith in God.

This fanciful scenario is not as far-fetched as you might think. These are the very presents Paul asks God to give to believers. I call them presents because Paul views every good thing we have from God as a gift, an illustration of His grace toward us, more evidence of His kindness.

So if you already have these qualities, I assume you will want to do everything that I mentioned above. And if you "open" these gifts in a moment to come, I will expect to hear your shouts and songs and laughter.

May God give peace to you,
my Christian brothers, and love, with faith from
God the Father and the Lord Jesus Christ.

EPHESIANS 6:23

65

Live Fully—And Don't
Fear Death

HAVE YOU NOTICED that real "giants" of the faith seem to develop a deep sense of inner peace about their future—even about their own death?

I have known several spiritual giants, and each of them had this same attribute. They lived their lives fully but weren't frightened by the prospect of death. They wanted to help other people find the same kind of wholeness they had discovered. It meant the world to them.

I yearn to be one of those giants. Do you? Here's what I think is necessary if we want to grow in that direction:

1. We need to develop a deeply personal relationship with the God who empowers us through the Holy Spirit. This is what we mean by a "personal relationship with Jesus Christ." We actually experience ourselves encountered by a personal God who is deeply interested in all the details of our lives.

2. We need to take God so seriously that we recognize His overwhelming power—power over life and death, power over evil, power over every force that threatens to dominate us.

3. We need to believe that we will never be separated from the love of God. On a regular basis, we must read the passage in Romans 8 in which Paul talks about how convinced he is that nothing can separate us from this loving God.

4. We need to recognize that there is life after death—that God has a plan for us for all of eternity.

When we integrate these four strategies into our lives, we will move rapidly toward being spiritual giants. When we have achieved this level of spiritual maturity, we will no longer worry about living and dying. That will be a minor issue! We will do everything in our power to help other people get into this same kind of life-changing relationship with our risen Lord.

> *For to me, living means opportunities for Christ, and dying—well, that's better yet! But if living will give me more opportunities to win people to Christ, then I really don't know which is better, to live or die!*
>
> PHILIPPIANS 1:21–22

66

Open Your Heart
to Peace

A FRIEND OF MINE, Dr. Vaughn Starnes, is one of the great heart surgeons of the world. He cares for people who have heart ailments of various kinds—people we might call the "brokenhearted." And when patients' hearts become damaged beyond repair, my friend gives them new ones.

He operates on both children and adults, and his incredible success and world-class standing are due to his unbelievable surgical skill. When I asked another heart doctor of some renown why my friend is so unusually proficient, he said, "He has such skillful hands that he can tie knots with invisible thread."

His prominence throughout the world is enhanced by the fact that we place such importance on the human heart. The heart, of course, has for years been considered the center of the inner life. While we now know that the real center of our inner life resides in our brains, we still communicate crucial things to one another through the use of the "heart" metaphor.

When the apostle Paul speaks about "peace of heart," he refers to the deepest experience available to us. He encourages us to seek after the kind of peace that will pervade our lives. It is the peace of heart that comes only through Christ.

Why is this so? Because when it comes to the *spiritual* heart, only Christ has what it takes to tie knots with invisible thread. He is the one who loves us when we are unlovely. He is the one who binds us up. He is the one who pursues us when we have run away from Him, and He consistently lets us know how dear we are to Him.

When you find the peace of heart that the apostle Paul talks about, you will experience a centeredness, an "insyncness" that you have never known before. It will be the exact inner condition your soul has thirsted for all your life.

Let the peace of heart which comes from Christ be always present in your hearts and lives.

COLOSSIANS 3:15

67

Work Hard to Be a
Great Father

I WENT TO lunch last week with our oldest grandson, Matt, and his father, Greg Forgatch. The three of us celebrated Matt's ninth birthday by going to the restaurant of his choice, the Soup Plantation.

Greg had driven by Matt's school and gotten him out of class, much to his delight. And then the two of them swung by my office to pick me up.

About two hours later when they dropped me off, I thought, *That was one of the most enjoyable times I've had in recent months.* One of the most impressive aspects of the experience was catching an up-close glimpse of a great father raising his son.

Marylyn and I had given Matt as a birthday present a small electronic device like the one I always carry. It has an alarm clock, a calculator, and it can be programmed to store twenty-three names and telephone numbers. The device allows you to press buttons to create a representative face next to each person's name.

Matt unwrapped the gift and admired it as much as he could, considering he didn't yet know its capabilities.

"Thanks, Grandpa," he said. "Looks like fun . . . what can it do exactly?"

That's when his dad got active. Greg leafed through the instruction booklet, read parts of it to Matt, and helped him follow the points. It wasn't long until Matt had the name of his cousin and closest friend, Patrick McGowan, stored in the device, along with Patrick's telephone number and a picture.

"This is so cool!" he nearly shouted. "What else can it do, Dad?"

Greg began to let Matt do more and more of the work, careful to get involved only when Matt had a question. Within a few minutes, Matt had set the correct time, entered several of his friends' names, and he seemed to be thoroughly enjoying himself.

"Hey, Matt, that's great," Greg said. "You've got that all figured out."

I had a ball watching these two interact. And though this may seem like a relatively minor event, it was an example of great parenting in action. Think of all the things Greg did to make Matt's day so special. He picked him up at school and took him to his favorite restaurant. He got involved with him in opening a fun, new present. He helped him in every way he could. He backed off and let his son take over when Matt was able. And he offered encouragement for his son's persistence.

I've noted that Greg fathers his four boys this way virtually all the time.

Now and then, the boys push the boundaries—as all boys do. And Greg is not afraid to give them a time-out and let them know he is displeased with them. He has just the right amount of correction in his voice—never too much and seldom too little.

And I have never heard him put them down in a way that discouraged them and made them quit trying.

If we could help every man who has children to become a father like Greg, what an incredible asset that would be for this nation's children—and for society at large. For there is something in being fathered well that gives children the inner confidence to be strong and self-reliant through all the difficulties of life.

Fathers, don't scold your children so much that they become discouraged and quit trying.

COLOSSIANS 3:21

68

Discover the Secret of Mutual Submission

TWO OR THREE years ago, I wrote to friends and colleagues all over the country and asked them to nominate the healthiest marriage they knew for a book I was writing. I ended up with spouses in one hundred extremely healthy marriages, and I asked these two hundred persons everything I could think of about how they became so successful.

Although nearly all of them said something wonderfully positive about their spouse, I detected something even deeper about these great marriages. It seemed to me that what these persons had learned to do was to "surrender" to each other. They actually seemed to yield themselves to the authority or will of each other. In essence, they submitted to each other.

This is exactly what God says to do through the words of the apostle Paul. It's not something we always want to do, that's for sure! When your spouse presents an idea that you don't like, it's easy to retort, "You're nuts! We're not doing that!" When your partner feels strongly about carrying through on some plan, it's easy to adamantly refuse rather than saying, "Help me to understand where you're coming from."

Great marriages involve a lot of give-and-take, a lot of compromising and adapting. And if one person submits lovingly, the other person is more likely to submit in response. Of course, there's a danger here. If a pattern emerges in which one individual gives in too often, that isn't good for either of the partners.

But what is good is when both of them participate in a process designed to bring resolution to every difference they have. I have a five-step model that I teach all the couples who come to me for therapy. It works like magic when it is used consistently:

1. Each partner has a perfect right to his or her thoughts and feelings, even if these thoughts and feelings are different from the other person's.

2. Each partner has an enormous need to have his or her thoughts and feelings accurately understood.

3. Whatever the difference is between them, it needs to be precisely identified so that it doesn't get blown out of proportion. In other words, if the two partners have different ideas about how to spend a vacation, they should pinpoint exactly what the difference is.

4. Then the crucial element, "mutual submission," is enacted. Something like this needs to be said: "Okay now, honey, how can I change on this and how can you change on it so we can come to an agreement that's acceptable to both of us?"

5. The partners need to celebrate every time a conflict gets resolved this way. They need to "high-five" one another.

This model promotes a spirit of mutual respect and honor, of viewing each other as having something important to say about every conflict, and of treating each other with dignity. I know from hundreds of cases that it works. It is a time-honored truth that comes straight from God Himself.

Honor Christ by submitting to each other.

EPHESIANS 5:21

69

Learn to Trust—and Watch Your Life Become Richer

IF JESUS IS GOD, and if He has power over every other force in the world, then the only thing for us to do is to trust in Him.

It is the experience of *trust* that sets you free. When you trust God, everything about your life becomes more joyful and more manageable. A big load is lifted off your back.

When you place your trust in Christ, you sense that you can afford to be openly and entirely yourself. That's because trust makes possible the reduction of defensiveness—that is, you don't feel a need to protect yourself from judgment, abandonment, or personal attack. Being free from defensiveness allows each person's true self ample opportunity for expression.

Similarly, when you develop trust in your primary earthly relationships, you change everything about them, too. For instance, marriages in which two people trust each other at the deepest levels have at least five priceless assets. First, they have emotional insurance that provides support and stability through all the hard times of life. You think this isn't worth much? Ask the people who have been through a few difficult periods. Ask them if it mattered much that the person they loved was there with them for as long as the hard times lasted. I suspect that it mattered more than they can say with mere words.

Second, these married people know that they can go all out in their quest to maximize their potential as individuals. They don't have to worry about failure. If they fail, their companion won't reject them or abandon them. They know they can lean on the unconditional faithfulness of their partner.

Third, they don't have to expend their time or energy being suspicious. There isn't any need to second-guess their lover. What this person says to them is truthful. There are total freedom and total trust.

Fourth, they are assured that every investment they make in this partnership will pay dividends. They know their marriage will last, so all the effort that goes into making it strong will reap rich rewards.

Finally, they can have genuine peace of mind. When you fully trust your partner, when there is absolutely no need for suspicion of any kind, when abandonment is totally out of the question, you can have one of the greatest prizes in the world—peace of mind.

Trust is at the center of the internal process in which we become fully free to actualize all the potential God has given to us. This trust always starts with reliance on God. Then we can implement it in our closest relationships— and watch our lives become more meaningful, productive, and enjoyable.

The source of all this trust? Jesus the Christ!

> *Because of his kindness you have been saved*
> *through trusting Christ. And even trusting is not of*
> *yourselves; it too is a gift from God.*
>
> EPHESIANS 2:8

70

Ensure the Health of Your Marriage by Submitting Properly

THROUGHOUT RECORDED HISTORY, there has been considerable concern about Paul's admonition that wives should submit to their husbands. Some people view this encouragement by Paul as a cultural matter. They argue: "That was fine for a Jewish culture two thousand years ago, but times have changed! We don't treat women this way anymore."

True, I have seen some terrible cases in which women have been expected to submit to men whose emotional health was so poorly developed that they should not have been in a position of leadership in *any* marriage. But as a psychologist, I recognize the crucial importance of what Paul has to say. You may disagree with me on this, but at least hear me out.

If you've read the previous chapters in this book, you know that Paul desperately wants *everyone* to experience freedom, peace, and contentment. So there is no reason to think he would advocate submission as a way to suppress, hinder, or hamper someone. No, Paul intends for submission—employed properly—to benefit not only the marriage, but both individuals as well.

I believe three criteria must be met in order for submission to contribute to the health of a marriage:

1. First, the husband must show the same kind of love to his wife "as Christ showed to the church when he died for her" (Ephesians 5:25). He must love sacrificially and be willing to give himself up for his most precious person, his wife. He needs to *really* love her!

2. The husband must "honor Christ by submitting" to his wife (Ephesians 5:21). If this mutual submission has not occurred, it must be viewed as a serious violation of a prior instruction.

3. The husband must be emotionally sound, free of any kind of addiction, with his anger under full control. In other words, submission must never be used to the detriment or harm of the wife.

These three criteria are necessary to ensure the stability and well-being of the marriage. And when a marriage is healthy, a husband can assume his leadership role. Clearly, it is a sacrificial kind of leadership. He becomes a servant.

This kind of a man listens carefully to his wife, honors her by trying hard to understand her, and is willing to give his very life for her. In response to him, she submits herself to his leadership in the same way she submits to the Lord.

All of this must be worked out with great care and concern. It is a delicate matter. But Paul has made this teaching crystal clear. We dare not ignore its value.

You wives must submit
to your husbands' leadership in the same way
you submit to the Lord.

EPHESIANS 5:22

71

Love Your Wife with Your Life

SAM AND MARTHA are friends of mine, and Martha told me recently that she thinks she's the most loved person she knows. But, she hastened to add, it hasn't always been that way.

Sam grew up in New York City, in a troubled family where conflict raged regularly. He was close to his mother but constantly frustrated with his eccentric, untrustworthy father. For his part, Sam was assertive, bright, and determined to succeed. When he and Martha met, he was a hard-charging young lawyer in the law firm that her father had cofounded.

Martha's upbringing was quite different from Sam's. Her parents were soft-spoken, kind, and seemingly free of conflicts. Martha can't ever recall observing a family fight.

Partly because of the background differences, the first few years of Sam and Martha's marriage were like a roller-coaster ride. Sam's shoot-from-the-hip style was dominating and, at times, uncontrollable. He seldom exploded and he never physically threatened his wife in any way, but his conflict style was loud and forceful. In contrast, Martha's approach to disagreements was quiet, gentle, and soft.

And then everything changed.

Ten years into their marriage, Martha was in a terrible accident. During a snowstorm, the bus she was riding in was broadsided by a speeding train. She spent the next several weeks in the hospital, listed in critical condition. Throughout those agonizing weeks, Sam wouldn't leave her bedside. He prayed passionately for her recovery and channeled all his energy into helping her through.

Martha recovered, and both of them say their relationship changed dramatically because of that brush with death. Sam tells of sitting by his wife's hospital bedside night after night, thinking that she was the best thing that ever happened to him. Recognizing how devastating it would be to lose her, he began for the first time to look seriously at faith issues.

"I prayed, I bargained with God, I came face-to-face with my Lord," Sam says. "And I made Him a promise: 'I will love my wife like I know You have always loved me. Please, God, just let her live.'"

As Martha regained full strength, she became aware that Sam was a different man. He was considerably more reflective, and his wildness had mellowed. Everything about the way he treated his wife softened—including his style of relating to her during difficult times. He always remembered to honor her even when they disagreed, and he listened long and hard when they saw things in different ways. He became a gentle, compassionate husband.

And when Martha told me that she thinks she's "the most loved person she knows," it occurred to me that every woman, being loved this way by her man, would be inspired to give everything she had to the relationship.

From my point of view, great marriages always start with husbands who learn how to love sacrificially. No husband wants to have to sit at the bedside of his critically ill wife to come to that strong inner conviction. No man wants to have to plead, "Please, God, just let her live."

May we learn the importance of love long before we face the devastating possibility of losing the person who is our dearest friend and our greatest support. Consider for just a moment what your life would be like without your loved one—and then take time to express just how much that person means to you.

*And you husbands, show the same
kind of love to your wives as Christ showed to
the Church when he died for her.*

EPHESIANS 5:25

72

Sing Together

I GREW UP attending a little country church in Iowa. I don't think we ever had more than a hundred people in church on a Sunday morning, but numbers didn't matter. I remember that we just *loved* being together. And the thing we enjoyed doing the most was singing.

On Sunday afternoons, we would get together and sing for hours. We sang every kind of gospel song, and when we finished one, I could hardly wait for the next one. In my teens when I was learning to sing bass, I especially enjoyed the songs in which the basses took the lead. There weren't many of us basses, so I sang out with everything I had.

Sometimes even now—all these years later—I wish I could go back and spend a whole afternoon singing song after song with those wonderful people.

What is it about singing together that creates such a bond for a group? It seems as though our emotions are expressed much more fully through song than through the spoken word. When you put a tune to any message, and when you sing that message with passion and conviction, it communicates the most deeply held parts of you.

Intimacy on a group level is most often developed through singing. What intimacy is all about, of course, is the communication of our innermost feelings, beliefs, and concerns. As we share these deep parts of us, we weave ourselves together. Real bonding occurs!

So if any group of people wants to be woven together, they should sing! The more the group sings together, the closer they will feel. They will be sharing their hearts with one another, and they will end up being fused in a way that they have never been before.

Talk with each other much about the Lord, quoting
psalms and hymns and singing spiritual songs,
making music in your hearts to the Lord.

EPHESIANS 5:19

73

Practice the Art of Praising and Honoring Your Husband

I'VE KNOWN THOUSANDS of men and women in marriages that range from painful to wonderful. Some of the wonderful marriages spring immediately to my mind.

A couple in Minnesota named Lee and Emily have worked as hard on their marriage as any I have ever seen, and their relationship with each other and their relationships with their children are as healthy as human relationships can be.

I'll never forget what Emily said to me: "There are certain 'bedrock' qualities and strengths I saw in Lee, even during our courtship, that are still a part of him today. These qualities are deeper and stronger now, more distilled by the action of life's experiences and growing faith. I've seen him in all kinds of situations with many different types of people, and my love and respect for him continue to grow. I'm so blessed and so proud to be his wife."

Lee happens to be a prominent American leader, and he

has influenced the lives of thousands of people. Think how much more powerful his life is because of the respect and honor he receives from his wife.

Obviously, in order to have this kind of respect and honor, a wife needs to marry a good man. That's why it is so critical to marry someone you can respect and honor for the rest of your life. But even when the man is not perfect, a great wife knows how to help him move toward greatness. Nothing helps more with this than praising and honoring him for every virtue she sees in him.

As I travel around the country conducting relationship seminars, I never cease talking about the discovery that B. F. Skinner made many years ago at Harvard University: "If you reward someone for something that is good, he will move more and more in the direction of the ideal, but if you punish him for something that is bad, he will remain stagnant at the original level."

So I say to women whenever I have a chance, "Your love for your husband will be shown most effectively in the way you relate to him, the attitude you hold toward him. If you praise him and honor him every chance you have, you will contribute to his development as the kind of husband you will always admire at the deepest of levels."

And the wife must see to it that she deeply respects her husband—obeying, praising and honoring him.

EPHESIANS 5:33

74

❧

Let Your "Lifeguard"
Save You

YEARS AGO AT Huntington Beach, California, I came
perilously close to drowning. Along with some other over-
confident young men, I was swimming in the ocean, and I
greatly overestimated my ability to handle the complex
currents of that well-known area. I swam out too far to
begin with, and the powerful currents took me even farther. Using all the strength I could muster, I paddled and
kicked in the direction of the beach—and got nowhere.

After a half hour of treading water and watching the
shoreline move farther and farther away, I was exhausted
and nearly panicked. I had only a few minutes—maybe
even seconds—before I would have gone down to a tragic
death. I was *totally* incapable of saving myself.

That's when Don Rowan, the brother of my closest
friend, came swimming toward me. He wrapped his arm
under my chin, and he began paddling toward the shore.
He said, "Just relax, Neil, and everything will be okay." In

my desperate struggle, I could not have imagined more comforting words.

A minute or two later, a lifeguard saw what was happening and came to help. Before I knew it, I was lying on a towel, facedown, beginning to gain awareness of the near-death experience I had just been through. Until then, I had not allowed myself to consciously consider my own death.

And through the hours that followed, one thing kept reverberating over and over in my brain: "I was *totally* incapable of saving myself."

That's exactly the way it is for us in life. For whatever reason, we all get ourselves entangled in so many unhealthy relationships that there is no way for us to become whole, to become "saved" from all that fragmentation we experience when we try to please everyone in our lives. We are trapped! We are hopelessly confused about who we are and what the real goal is for our lives.

At this point, we need to know that we are lovable on the basis of God's grace and mercy. If He really loves us unconditionally, then and only then can we move toward the shore and get ourselves on emotionally solid ground again.

Amazingly, Christ swims toward us, puts His arm under our chin, tells us to relax, and saves us from drowning in our own confusion.

We Christians glory in what Christ Jesus has done for
us and realize that we are helpless to save ourselves.

PHILIPPIANS 3:3

75

Form an Alliance with
Your Spouse

LAST YEAR, a young couple I'll call Alan and Melissa came to me for marriage counseling. At the first session, I asked how they handled conflict.

"Well, here's an example," Alan said. "A few weeks ago, Melissa ran up a huge debt on our credit card. So I told her, 'If you can't control your spending, I'll hold on to all of our credit cards.'"

"And how did you respond to that, Melissa?" I asked.

"I said that was ridiculous!" she replied. "I mean, who doesn't go overboard on a shopping spree every now and then?"

Alan shot her a look that said, *Go on. Tell the rest of the story.*

"So then I called my mom and explained the situation," Melissa continued. "She said I was absolutely right!"

Even though I maintained a neutral expression, I thought, *Oh, boy. Not good.*

"What happened next?" I asked.

"What happens often—too often," Alan put in. "Melissa's mom and dad came over for a 'little chat.' They proceeded to give us all kinds of advice on money management. And, of course, my mother-in-law made a few not-so-subtle remarks about equality in marriage."

I wish I could report that Alan and Melissa's case was a rarity. Unfortunately, I counsel many couples whose parents are overly involved in their kids' marriage. And I always get nervous when I learn that a newlywed has "called home" and told his or her parents everything about their marital issues. It isn't a good sign! The husband and wife—by themselves—must figure out how to live together, solve problems, and communicate deeply. Parents should have absolutely no voting rights in their children's marriage.

Maybe I was lucky. My mother always took Marylyn's side if she heard about any problem in our marriage. I didn't tell her much, but if she got wind of some issue, she always came to me and "required" that I be good to Marylyn.

I've realized that our three daughters either have fabulous marriages or they have formed alliances with their husbands never to say anything about their issues to their parents. Wouldn't you think that a daughter whose father is a psychologist could "consult" him about a few marriage matters? Not our daughters!

Of course, that's the way it should be. Show me a

marriage in which the parents of the wife or husband meddle and tamper, and I will show you a marriage in trouble. It makes you want to say to the man or woman, "You're married now! Leave and cleave!"

In fact, that's close to what the apostle Paul says to married couples. In essence, he tells spouses, "Leave your father and mother so you can form a solid union with your mate. The two of you should forge a powerful bond."

If you want to have a marriage that's a thousand times easier and richer, leave your parents out of any issue you and your spouse are confronting. Resolve the problem between the two of you—and reap the satisfaction of knowing you've made your relationship stronger and healthier.

> *A man must leave his father and mother when*
> *he marries, so that he can be perfectly joined*
> *to his wife, and the two shall be one.*
>
> EPHESIANS 5:31

76

Honor Your Father and Mother and Experience the Great Promise

ANY FAMILY THAT frequently and enthusiastically honors the mother and father is one with *tremendous potential.*

My parents were happily married for more than seventy
years. My two sisters and I, along with our extended family, got together year after year to honor this great mother
and father. We gathered at parks for picnics, attended
church events together, and we held parties and receptions
for their friends and neighbors. We were so proud of them!
We wanted to honor them in every way we knew how.

And each of us has received the reward Paul talks about
for those who treat their parents with deference and
respect—we have lived long lives, full of blessing.

What about your family? Do you have a mother and
father you enjoy honoring? If your dad really loves your
mom as Christ loves the church, and if your mom honors
and respects your dad like a loving Christian wife, I imagine that you enjoy honoring both of them.

❦

Some families are not quite so fortunate. Their dad and mom don't get along very well, and they are not so easy to honor—or even tolerate. I always encourage persons in families like this to find whatever they can that is worthy of honor and then to give that honor as freely as possible. Where this is not possible, I encourage these persons to commit themselves with all their hearts to making sure that they become far different parents so that their children can honor them with enthusiasm.

The apostle Paul says that forming strong family relationships is one of the best ways to enjoy life and withstand the troubles this world throws at you. Then he encourages us to play vital roles in the family-building process. Men are to be great leaders, deeply loving, patient, and sacrificial. Women are to be supportive, helpful partners of this kind of man. Children are to obey, honor, and respect their parents.

And when all of this happens the way it should, what a difference it makes for every family member.

Obey your parents; this is the right thing
to do because God has placed them in authority
over you . . . And this is the promise: that if you
honor your father and mother, yours will
be a long life, full of blessing.

EPHESIANS 6:1, 3

77

Treat Your Kids with
Great Dignity

AFTER ALL THESE years of listening to parents talk
about their children, I've become convinced that most of
their passion revolves around the mystery represented by
the blending of both spouses' physical, emotional, and
intellectual qualities. It's the magical combination of "half
my genes and half yours."

There is something mind-boggling about the idea that
the love of my life and I can somehow merge our unique-
ness—our very beings—in a little person who will live
with us and be around us for the rest of our lives. And this
little being will be an incredible blend of you and me. We
can have a little *us*.

I remember the birth of our first child as if it were yesterday. Lorrie was born after we had been at the hospital
for only forty minutes, and she was wide awake, pink and
white, and more beautiful than anything I had ever seen in
my life. I watched her being given her first "shower," and

then I went down to see Marylyn as they were bringing her back from the delivery room. Still groggy, she looked up at me and asked if everything was all right.

I immediately blurted out, "We have the most magnificent little girl I've ever seen!"

Even in her grogginess, Marylyn squealed with delight. I hugged her, and we cried together. We both recall this moment as the most inspirational experience of our entire marriage. It was our first taste of "half my genes and half yours." When you encounter the mystery of human life from such an up close vantage point, you cannot fail to sense the powerful presence of God.

It occurs to me that this extraordinary experience needs to be played and replayed in our minds and in our family "story times" as frequently as possible. This will keep us relating to our children so much more positively. It will eliminate the negative, frustrated conversations that go nowhere. When we remember what a treasure our children are, we will treat them with great dignity.

And when we do, their lives will bud and blossom as at no other time. Families that continually point out the deficiencies, irregularities, and inadequacies of their children produce little boys and girls who are stifled and insecure. But families that consistently hug their children and affirm all that is good and right about them end up with boys and girls who stand a good chance of becoming all that God created them to be.

One of the most important things we can do to make

our lives better and richer is to treat our children with the kind of dignity with which God treats us.

And now a word to you parents.
Don't keep on scolding and nagging your children,
making them angry and resentful.

EPHESIANS 6:4

78

Delight in
Each Passing Moment

FIFTEEN YEARS AGO, our three daughters introduced
Marylyn and me to singer James Taylor, whom we have
thoroughly enjoyed ever since. J. T.'s song "Secret o' Life"
is by far my favorite of all his recordings. In this song, he
says that the secret of life is to enjoy the passing of time.

As I've thought about this principle, I've concluded that
there are three secrets to enjoying the passing of time:

1. You need to be crystal clear about your position in
   the context of creation. For instance, you need to
   know who has created you, what He has in mind for
   you, how He wishes to be involved with you, and
   what your ultimate purpose is within His creative
   scheme.

2. You need to understand and appreciate your unique-
   ness. To get the most out of your time on earth, you

must be highly differentiated as a human being. This means that you "deeply discover" yourself—all your interests, skills, gifts, strengths, and weaknesses—and you come to highly value the person you are. If you know precisely who you are, the confusion and uncertainty of your life will vanish.

3. You need to surround yourself with healthy persons who hold values similar to your own. If you are a Christian, you need to be around people who understand and practice unconditional love, who are free to be authentic and genuine, and who serve others in a spirit of charity and generosity.

If these three criteria are met, you are sure to enjoy the passing of your time. You will not be compelled to look back at missed opportunities or past glories, nor will you constantly long for a better situation ahead. You can savor your life as it unfolds. You can delight in each passing moment.

For I can do everything God asks me to with the help of Christ who gives me the strength and power.

PHILIPPIANS 4:13

79

Choose the Right "Guidance System" for Your Life

THE APOSTLE PAUL tells us that two conflicting guidance systems seek to direct our ways. The first is what he calls "your own wrong inclinations." These inclinations inevitably lead to fragmentation and brokenness.

The other guidance system is the Holy Spirit. Paul advises you to "obey only the Holy Spirit's instructions. He will tell you where to go and what to do, and then you won't always be doing the wrong things your evil nature wants you to" (Galatians 5:16). According to the New Testament, when Jesus left the earth, He gave us the Comforter, the Counselor, the very presence of God. When the Holy Spirit fills you, it is as if Jesus Himself takes the helm of your life and navigates your course.

When you elect the guidance system called the Holy Spirit, your life moves in the right direction. You are filled with the powerful sense of being deeply loved, since *everything* about Jesus' teaching focuses on love. Moreover, you become identified with Jesus. You take on His power, His glory, His mission. You feel good about your purpose for being. You know you have enormous worth as a human being. You know exactly how to become satisfied at your deepest levels.

One consequence of allowing this Guide to direct your path is that you feel peaceful with the people in your life. As a matter of fact, Paul indicates that this may be the most important consequence of being filled with the Holy Spirit. Paul is deeply concerned about your relationships with others—especially with other believers in Christ.

What a phenomenal gift! *You* can tap into the power of the Holy Spirit. And when you do, you will feel so good about yourself that you will want to pursue peace with your family, your friends, your business associates, your fellow workers, and even your enemies.

As you move through life, be sure your ways are directed by the right guidance system—and then thoroughly enjoy the journey.

*Try always to be led along together by the Holy
Spirit, and so be at peace with one another.*

EPHESIANS 4:3

80

Let Your Life Be Transfused
with Peace

DO YOU HAVE peace within yourself?

If not, can you put your finger on why you don't? Is one of your primary relationships not going well? Are you "out of sync" with a parent or child, your spouse, a close friend, a supervisor, or an employee?

Or are you worried about financial matters? Have debts piled up? Is your mailbox full of bills while your checking account is empty? Are you wondering how you'll pay next month's rent?

Or maybe you feel that your life is going nowhere. You've spent years in school and you've worked hard, but you still feel that you're stuck in neutral. How will you ever get where you want to be?

Obviously, all of these issues are critical. When we have problems like these, we naturally become greatly concerned. This concern is designed to motivate us to do whatever we must to get these issues dealt with adequately.

Still, we can be at peace even in *the midst of difficult* struggles. In other words, you don't have to have all your problems solved in order to experience tranquillity and calm. Regardless of the trouble you face, your life can be transfused with serenity.

The apostle Paul cared more about our developing peace than he cared about almost anything else. During the time he wrote Galatians, Ephesians, Philippians, and Colossians, he was in prison because of his beliefs. Confined and probably in chains, he still experienced the kind of deep peace he wanted for each of his readers.

In the first two or three verses of each of these epistles, Paul talks about this peace. In Galatians 1:3, he says: "May peace and blessing be yours from God the Father and from the Lord Jesus Christ." In Ephesians 1:2, he says: "May his blessings and peace be yours." In Philippians 1:2, he says: "I pray that God our Father and the Lord Jesus Christ will give each of you his fullest blessings, and his peace in your hearts and your lives." And finally, in Colossians 1:2, he says: "May God our Father shower you with blessings and fill you with his great peace."

Surely, many of Paul's readers were in the middle of economic problems, relational frustrations, health concerns, church power struggles, complex national difficulties, and on and on. But Paul prayed that they would be peaceful—even as they were buffeted by these troubles.

If you want this kind of peace, you can have it. You simply need to ask the God of all creation to fill you with

Himself, to give you deep-down certainty that you are within His care, to provide for you now and throughout eternity.

There is *nothing* like this peace. It will turn your pain into the raw materials for personal growth. It will transform your relational struggles into opportunities for progress. It will completely dissolve your anxiety.

May his blessings and peace be yours.

EPHESIANS 1:2

81

❧

Make a Peace Accord with
Your Enemies

DO YOU HAVE any enemies? I'd be surprised if you
don't, and actually, I hope you do. If you're standing
strong for things that really matter, some people are sure
to oppose you.

As a psychologist, I encourage every human being to
make choices for himself or herself. If I sense that *someone
else* is trying to usurp the decision-making right of a person
with whom I am working, I encourage my client to fend off
the "controllers." In the process, the people being fended off
often become angry with me for instigating this action. They
"hate" me for "coming between them and the person they
love—and the person they have had freedom to control."

So I have some enemies!

During biblical times, Jews and Gentiles were frequently pitted against one another. They were adversaries.
And since the time of Christ, Jews and Christians have
often been enemies.

That is why Paul's admonitions about peace are so important. According to Paul, all of us, whether Jews or Gentiles, "may come to God the Father with the Holy Spirit's help because of what Christ has done for us" (Ephesians 2:18).

When you're thinking about your enemies, remember that God is just as concerned about them as He is about you. Because God wants a relationship with you *and* your enemies, He encourages you to be as eager for their wholeness as He is for yours.

The most efficient way to bring about peace between you and your adversaries is to remember three simple facts:

1. The same God who created you created them, and He loves you both equally.

2. Peace is established between two persons when they both recognize that their worth is firmly established, that their future is secure, and their importance to God will never diminish.

3. When this *intra*personal love gets converted into *inter*personal love, when the two foes become motivated to improve their relationship, wonderful things begin to happen.

When you stand firm on your beliefs and live according to your convictions, you are bound to make people angry with you at some point. What's important is how you respond when others oppose you. You can fan the flames of hostility or you can pursue peace. Remember Paul's principle: Every person on earth can live in the peace that comes from God through Christ.

And he has brought this Good News of peace
to you Gentiles who were very far away from
him, and to us Jews who were near.

EPHESIANS 2:17

82

Bring Up Your Children with Loving Discipline

I HAVE WATCHED thousands of parents interact with their children, and I've often had the opportunity to see how these relationships turned out. In the process, I have gained a strong sense of what works and what doesn't work. Here is my list of seven parenting principles for the development of great kids.

Principle #1: Your child is a separate being. Successful parents tell me that no other principle is as important as this one. As a parent, you are a "trustee." Your children are not *you,* and you are not your *children.* You have them for only a short while, and then they will make their way in the world.

This means, of course, that you should not try to make them into a carbon copy of yourself. They have a separate identity, they are created with a different genetic makeup from any person on earth, they have unique personalities, and they will ultimately determine their own destiny.

Principle #2: You have been entrusted with the sacred task of helping your children become everything they are capable of becoming. A fundamental part of your parenting task is to help your children discover their talents, strengths, interests, gifts, and natural abilities. This discovery process requires lots and lots of listening on the part of parents. It also takes keen observation, as you watch and determine where your child's natural talents lie. Once identified, these talents must be nurtured and cultivated.

Principle #3: Vital to your children's development is a consistent experience of being loved unconditionally. Absolutely nothing is more important to psychological development than children's receiving assurance that their worth is never in jeopardy, that they are loved simply because of who they are—not on the basis of any conditional factors. Love shouldn't be given and taken away because of behavior, performance, intellect, appearance, academic achievement, or any other component.

Principle #4: Parents must carefully determine and consistently maintain limits for their children. These limits give their children a sense of security, and they protect both the parents and others from out-of-control children.

I recommend that parents spend generous amounts of time determining proper boundaries for their children, that they seek the best advice they can, and work hard to agree on what these limits should be. Once established, these boundaries should be consistently enforced.

❦

Principle #5: Parents must decide how to discipline their children in the most effective way. Discipline is absolutely vital to the formation of great kids—and the formation of great parent-child relationships. But the exact methods of discipline that parents should adopt are something only they can determine.

Principle #6: Parents should help their children dream a big dream for their lives. Parents are in a prime position to help their children develop a dream. Just as parents need a dream for their marriage and their own lives, so do children need a big vision for what they can become. This dream can be modified all along the way, but any dream will stimulate their brains and mobilize their action centers.

Principle #7: Parents must help their children develop strong character and healthy values. I know of nothing so gratifying for parents as recognizing that their children have developed character attributes that will strengthen them for a lifetime. Likewise, when children identify values in which they passionately believe and for which they are willing to give their all, the parents can be deeply thankful and proud.

If you take the apostle Paul's instruction seriously, you will combine love and discipline in raising your children. When you do, the prize will be overwhelming. Show me great kids, and I will show you parents who have loved them and disciplined them with great care. What a sense of achievement for everyone involved.

❦

Bring [children] up with
the loving discipline the Lord himself approves,
with suggestions and godly advice.

EPHESIANS 6:4

83

Rehearse the Fact of
Your Salvation

THE APOSTLE PAUL makes it clear that all of us are weakened by our sin. The primary definition of sin he focuses on is, in the words of *Webster's Dictionary,* "a state of human nature in which the self is estranged from God."

He holds that our salvation is "a deliverance from the power and effects of this estrangement." It is when we are reconciled to God that we are *saved* from the effects of this estrangement.

When we are saved, we are freed to become the true persons we really are, the persons God created us with the capacity to be. Then we can become "whole," everything we truly are in our "saved state."

In this state of "salvation," we become highly alert to everything that would diminish or erode our wholeness. And we become powerful, because now we have our true nature, the nature God gave us, available.

It is because of this salvation that Paul can say that the Lord's mighty power works within us (Ephesians 6:10).

This wholeness, this salvation, is of paramount importance in our dealings with every temptation that comes our way. And a constant awareness of our personal salvation will have an enormous part to play in our victory over the challenging forces of the world.

And you will need the helmet of salvation.

EPHESIANS 6:17

84

Keep the Faith
When Times Get Hardest

ONE OF THE persons I deeply loved when I was a boy was the minister of our church, H. Frank Cope. Though he has been dead for many years, I think of him often. As a matter of fact, every time I hear from a family member or friend who mentions his name, I recall his unusual ability to use his faith as a shield.

My appreciation of Frank Cope began when I was ten years old. There was a couple at the church who had become frustrated with his leadership, and the harshness of their language toward him was a matter of public knowledge. Even as these people disparaged and maligned him—which they did often—he kept his cool and handled every situation skillfully. The more he managed those difficult situations with poise and equanimity, the more my admiration for him grew.

The only issue that seemed to matter to him was the truth. When his opponents attacked him personally, he didn't appear to be bothered. What was it that kept their sharp, biting tongues from wounding him? I'm confident it was his deep faith. How is it that faith could serve as a shield like this?

In the New Testament, *faith* is always connected to God. In other words, the Bible never advocates faith in self, faith in government, faith in nature, or faith in anything else. If you have true faith, you have faith *in God*.

And what is it that makes faith in God so powerful and reliable? What He has done historically. In the Old Testament, He always referred to what He had done for the children of Israel in leading them out of the land of bondage and across the Red Sea. And in the New Testament, God again proves His faithfulness by sending a savior—one who died for our sins and was raised from the dead.

When you have faith in God, what changes for you in relation to the difficulties you face? You *know* that your worth is never in question, that your value is established for all time, that your acceptance in God's eyes could never change. God loves you so much that He gave His only Son for you.

So when Frank Cope faced those attackers, he remained cool and composed. He listened to them, tried to find out exactly what concerned them, and fended off their personal attacks with the shield of faith.

Whenever you face a difficult interaction in your life, make sure you take the shield of faith with you. God Himself will be on your side, for He will assure you that there is nothing about the situation that can cause His acceptance of you to waver. And when you know that, you will be able to deal generously and kindly with every person. You will have credibility with all who hear, because it will be obvious that you are one of God's true believers.

In every battle you will need faith as your shield
to stop the fiery arrows aimed at you by Satan.

Ephesians 6:16

85

Unleash the Power
of God in You

THE LONGER I work as a psychologist the more impressed I become with the enormous power of the human personality. This power is unleashed when any human being gets into a right relationship with God—when he or she receives the love that sets them free from all of their entanglements with a difficult and conditional world.

When people believe in this loving, empowering God, when they immerse themselves in His grace, when they become personally related to Him, all of the power of their gifts becomes available to them.

The apostle Paul himself is a great example of this. What a powerful person Paul was. He was constantly under attack, repeatedly challenged, frequently imprisoned and whipped, and yet he is credited with the authorship of more New Testament books than any other person. He had more to do with the growth of the Christian faith than anyone but Jesus Himself.

How could this be? It's obvious! He had the mighty power of God unleashed within him and through him. There is no other explanation that makes sense.

Here was a person who was muffled in every way the world knew to muffle him, and yet he always emerged more confident and assured. You think Paul didn't face hardship? Consider his own words:

> I have . . . been put in jail oftener, been whipped times without number, and faced death again and again and again. Five different times the Jews gave me their terrible thirty-nine lashes. Three times I was beaten with rods. Once I was stoned. Three times I was shipwrecked. Once I was in the open sea all night and the whole next day. (2 Corinthians 11:23–25)

Paul goes on to tell all kinds of other trouble he experienced. His enemies said that he "turned the rest of the world upside down" (Acts 17:6). He won followers for Christ from every religion of his day. And his incredible writings still inspire enormous gratitude and action in all of us.

Throughout the books of Galatians, Ephesians, Philippians, and Colossians, Paul talks about the "mighty power of God" within his life.

If you want this mighty power, make sure you do what is necessary. Believe that Jesus *is* God. Trust Him to care for you and give you everything you need. Allow His Holy

Spirit to invade you and fill you full. And then ask God to unleash His power in you and through you.

This will make it possible for you to manage every circumstance of your life, resolve problems that have dogged you for years, turn troubled relationships into happy ones, and use your gifts and talents to their fullest.

The secret? God's mighty power in your life.

I want to remind you that your strength must come
from the Lord's mighty power within you.

EPHESIANS 6:10

About the Author

NEIL CLARK WARREN, PH.D., is a practicing clinical psychologist and the founder of Associated Psychological Services in Pasadena, California. The former dean of the Fuller Graduate School of Psychology, he is the author of *Finding the Love of Your Life, Make Anger Your Ally, The Triumphant Marriage,* and *Finding Contentment* (recently selected as a finalist in the Books for Better Living awards). Warren resides with his family in Pasadena, California.